CRAMPS

```
Have you ever tasted a rotten tomato
After an obese striped alley cat
cam along and
            peed
             on
             it!
And soon the acidic urine taste
              mi
               xes
           with the
           waking
        deterioration
And  the  red
      T H I C K
         skin
       transforms
          into a
       shriveled
           brown
           GLOB
            AND
            the
           brown
           liquid
          substance
           oozes
all over the sidewalk
           AND
        seconds later
        a    BIG
       STEAMROLLER
         comes along
           AND
     m  a  s  h  e  s
the tomato to oblivion
           AND
a construction crew working from a 16th storey building
              d
              r
              o
              p
              s
a piano on the suffering creation
           AND
15 little girls begin to play hopscotch
             on
             it!
            AND
one of the little girls in her blackpatentleather
shoes and white frilly socks
             s
              l
               i
                p
                 s

           AND
          falls
```

Don't Get Too Excited

Jenny Bagel

Don't Get Too Excited

It's Just About a

Pair of Shoes and

Other Laments

From My Life

JEN EPSTEIN

GREEN PLACE BOOKS | *Brattleboro, Vermont*

Printed in the United States

10 9 8 7 6 5 4 3 2 1

Green Writers Press is a Vermont-based publisher whose mission
is to spread a message of hope and renewal through the words and
images we publish. Throughout we will adhere to our commitment
to preserving and protecting the natural resources of the earth.
To that end, a percentage of our proceeds will be donated to
environmental activist groups and the author's charity of choice.
Green Writers Press gratefully acknowledges support from individual
donors, friends, and readers to help support the environment and
our publishing initiative. Green Place Books curates books that tell
literary and compelling stories with a focus on writing about place.

GREEN PLACE BOOKS   GREEN writers press

Giving Voice to Writers & Artists Who Will Make the World a Better Place
Green Writers Press | Brattleboro, Vermont
www.greenwriterspress.com

ISBN: 978-1-7320815-4-3

COVER DESIGN: Asha Hossain
BOOK DESIGN: Hannah Wood

PRINTED ON PAPER WITH PULP THAT COMES FROM FSC-CERTIFIED FORESTS, MANAGED FORESTS THAT GUAR-
ANTEE RESPONSIBLE ENVIRONMENTAL, SOCIAL, AND ECONOMIC PRACTICES BY LIGHTNING SOURCE. ALL WOOD
PRODUCT COMPONENTS USED IN BLACK AND WHITE, STANDARD COLOR OR SELECT COLOR PAPERBACK BOOKS,
UTILIZING EITHER CREAM OR WHITE BOOKBLOCK PAPER,, THAT ARE MANUFACTURED IN THE LAVERGNE, TEN-
NESSEE PRODUCTION CENTER ARE SUSTAINABLE FORESTRY INITIATIVE (SFI) CERTIFIED SOURCING.

To my mother

CONTENTS

PREFACE

It All Started
with a Pair of Shoes

For the past several years, "Don't get too excited" has been my quip about almost anything. It is the self-deprecating response that my friends, coworkers, family, mail carrier, and next-door neighbors—really anyone whom I cross paths with—have had the pleasure, or in some cases, the extreme misfortune, of hearing from me.

It all began in the fall of 2012, when two of my coworkers formed a writers group. At the time, my fellow employees knew me as a pragmatic problem solver who dealt with all the mundane, banal crap nobody else wanted to handle—like troubleshooting their technical issues and scheduling their orders. I'm sure, dear reader, as fellow worker bees of the twenty-first century, you know exactly what I mean by banal, mundane crap.

When I entered the conference room that October evening, I had no expectations that after sharing my piece, those perceptions would change. Before reading, I said, "Don't get too excited, it's just about a pair of shoes."

Thirty minutes before our group was to congregate for the first time, I had written four paragraphs on having to attend physical therapy and wear orthotics in my sneakers (I was recovering from plantar fasciitis). I had anticipated that my piece would be met by blank facial expressions, but, in fact, quite the opposite happened. I was instead met with laughter and facial expressions indicating that the group wanted to hear more, not less.

That day, when I listed off my childhood collection of the Converse All Stars I had owned—charcoal, hunter green, chocolate brown, basic black, every color except for bubble-gum pink and cream white—I realized I had written more than simply a silly homage to my shoes. I had written something that everyone else could relate to. I understood that by expressing my frustration over physical therapy and having to work to gain my strength back, by admitting defeat that I could no longer show off this signature staple of my wardrobe, what I was actually saying was that I was getting older, losing my identity, and that it scared the hell out of me. More than a simple ode to footwear, it was about the fears that we all experience as human beings at one time or another.

I owe a great debt of gratitude to writers group. Their enthusiasm and compassion created a safe space to bring many of the essays that make up this book to fruition. For example, multiple drafts of "I Hope I Didn't Lose You," the chapter on fighting with customer support, were read out loud in writers group before I began compiling my stories into this book. A few members even suggested recording a reading of the essay in one of our sound booths at work and submitting to various radio programs for inclusion in their podcasts.

When I experienced a major health crisis, writers group was there to listen to me read a detailed account of how I coped with illness and processed making changes to my lifestyle. This was one of the more difficult pieces to write. I would start, stop, then start again. I truly believe that if not for the encouragement and constructive feedback I received from members of the group, I might have taken the easy way out, refraining from starting again.

Every month for four years, I shared my life with this group, and each month, before sharing, I prefaced the reading with the words, "Don't get too excited, it's just about (*fill in the blank*)." You can insert almost anything; it's just about Zanzibar, aardvarks, or pumice stones. They all fit very nicely.

To the reader, I invite you in these next chapters to laugh, cry, gasp, roll your eyes, slam the book down, go take a walk, and maybe think really hard about whether you actually want to pick it up again. Explore all your reactions and more.

Just promise me one thing. Don't get too excited, it's just about a pair of shoes.

INTRODUCTION

Exotic Diseases, Electric Fences,
and Other Irrational Fears, Oh My!

There is only one thing in this world over which I don't allow myself to obsess: how I developed Obsessive Compulsive Disorder. I do not spend sleepless nights ruminating about it, or overanalyzing. What would be the point? It wouldn't change anything. So it is best to accept and move on. At least, that is what I have been told and what I frequently need to remind myself.

But if I were to allow myself to probe a little deeper, I would have quite a few theories. For starters, both of my parents were mental health professionals; my father was a clinical psychologist, my mother a social worker. This is one of two pieces of my personal history that have always fascinated my therapist, and it was one of the first details I revealed about my life when I walked into her office a little over thirteen years ago. I remember her words in reaction to this revelation almost verbatim: "So, you're the child of mental health professionals? I fear for my children, and how they may turn out, because I am one."

This could be interpreted as, *God I hope my kids don't end up in therapy. And if they do, I hope it isn't my fault. And if it is my fault, I hope they don't write a book about me and how I ruined their lives. And if they do write a book, I hope it's just compiled into a mammoth volume of journals that gets stuffed into a desk drawer and isn't published.*

Or maybe that's not what my therapist was implying at all, but rather what I project my family's reaction might be—their worry that the words from my mammoth volume of journals, removed from a desk drawer and entered onto these next hundred-plus pages, should happen to be spotted on a bookstore shelf.

Let me preface something before I go any further. I don't blame my parents for my OCD or any of my other "issues." My mom is probably reading this right now and bristling over the accusation, so I want to make sure that she hears me. In fact, if anything, I thank them for it. I would not be the wise, strong, funny, quirky, empathic human being I am today if not for the many experiences in my life that have shaped and challenged me to maintain my resilience.

However, I do believe that from the moment I shot out of my mother's womb and entered the world, my parents became inclined to scrutinize and seek diagnosis over every potentially problematic issue they sensed, beginning with being born with a small head to when I finally took my first steps, a clumsy gait.

By the time I entered nursery school, my fine motor skills appeared to be developing at a slower rate than my peers. I was unable to tie my shoes, had difficulty running, doing somersaults, or other physical activities. Not long after that, my mother took me for intensive sessions of occupational therapy to pinpoint and analyze every possible explanation for my stunted development. I was born in the late seventies and grew up in the eighties, when enrolling your kid in occupational therapy, and diagnosing and treating learning disabilities or psychological disorders wasn't as common as it is today.

I was a very self-aware child, who understood that there was something "different" about me in comparison to other kids in my class. I sensed my parents focusing on diagnosing and treating what might be wrong with me, rather than recognizing what I did well. And that focus made me nervous.

I also learned how to read late, but I was a quick study, enamored with language, inquisitive and insightful. I devoured every book placed in front of me. Although my letters were cryptically formed, and my handwriting could have been studied by forensic experts to identify future serial killers, I was a fluid writer and imaginative storyteller. But because I displayed a notable disparity between language ability and fine motor skills, as well as computation and syntax skills, my confidence waned while my anxiety progressed.

The types of things I worried about were not ones that other kids developed obsessive tendencies over. They were irrational fears that no one my age, or in some cases, any age at all, should ever need to be concerned about. Looking back, there were telltale signs that I might grow up to develop an anxiety disorder, obsessive compulsive disorder, and symptoms of depression.

When I was about seven or eight years old, my father began taking me into the city to Columbia University for an extensive battery of IQ and psychological testing. Once a week, my confidence would diminish as I was asked to hop, jump rope, run through obstacle courses, stack blocks, and maneuver puzzle pieces. Then it would be restored when I was shown a series of cards and asked to tell a story with them, or play word games. At the end of each session, like a rat able to locate the cheese at the end of a maze, I was rewarded, usually with food. Shrimp salad, Cherry Coke, and rice pudding, all my favorites, served as sweet and savory distractions that shielded me from asking too many questions.

At the conclusion of these sessions, I was diagnosed with learning disabilities. Specifically, PI, or Perceptually Impaired. This affliction made and continues to make tasks requiring fine motor coordination, such as buttoning a shirt or zipping a jacket, very difficult. I felt the effects at school during recess. I would become very anxious as I watched other kids from my class swing across the monkey bars with such ease. I couldn't do that; I knew I would fall off on the first rung. That made me jealous and sad, and so I didn't want to play at all, which freed up plenty more time to obsess and worry.

My sister, who was six and a half years older, also had been diagnosed with learning disabilities when she was young. But her difficulties were not as pronounced, and she developed ways to compensate at a much earlier age than I did, so my parents didn't focus on her problems as much as they did on mine. I think because my parents seemed to frame everything that I did through this lens, I, too, began to intently focus on my diagnosis. It became my identity. I struggled to see anything about myself and the person I was becoming that extended beyond it. As a result, the obsessive tendencies and irrational fears worsened.

At eight, I became particularly fixated on electric fences. Even though we lived miles from one, every time I spotted a sign that said "DANGER HIGH VOLTAGE!" out the window of the car, I was petrified. I was convinced that I would soon meet my untimely fate by electric shock. There was no explanation for why I became consumed with the scenario, but with OCD, there never really is a specific, rational explanation.

When I was nine, my parents divorced. At this point, I had already been seeing a therapist for a few years, one of my parent's colleagues. I was well versed in talking about my problems at length; it seemed second nature to me to add reconciling their divorce to a long list of discussion points. Had I been left alone with a DSM IV manual, the quintessential guide used by psychotherapists to understand and diagnose psychological disorders, I probably could have conducted the sessions myself: "Why don't you step outside and get some coffee? I'll have this all figured out by the time you get back."

While the divorce proceedings were being finalized, I lived with my mother. But at the time, I had a very close relationship with my father. I spent a lot of time with him, but it never felt like enough. I told both my parents on several occasions that my wish was to live with him, and not my mother.

This may have in part been due to an unusually marked aspect of my relationship with my father. At some point in my early years, he started seeing his patients in our home. He had a door built and an office constructed in back of the living room. I would often frequent his office to talk with him about falling off the monkey bars, or a television program that showed an electric fence that I had become anxious over. He would sit in the chair where he sat when seeing patients; I would sit on the couch that his patients would sit on during a session. With guidance from my therapist later in my adult life, I would begin to understand how inappropriate this was. Essentially, my father was acting as a therapist and treating his daughter as if she were his patient. Nevertheless, these "sessions" brought me great solace and temporary relief from my anxiety, forming what I believed at the time to be an unbreakable bond between us.

So when I was eleven, I moved in with him. My mother felt hurt over this rejection from her youngest child; all she wanted was for both of her children to be happy. This was a quality I would grow to admire deeply, but not long after I moved in with my father, I entered adolescence—and at a time in life when a child needs her mother, I didn't see much of mine, or of my sister, who was in high school and had her own life. My father was also preparing to get remarried.

This was when a new irrational fear cropped up. I became obsessed with an insignificant part of the human anatomy. Namely, my uvula, the little piece of lobe that hangs at the back of your throat. I was fascinated by what exactly its function was, but troubled that it appeared loose when I opened my mouth and watched it dangling and jiggling in the reflection of the bathroom mirror. I became convinced that this inconsequential orifice would detach and fall out when I least expected it. Even worse, I might swallow it. If my throat became dry and too much saliva built up, that thing might snap and break off like a twig. For months this was all I talked about. My father consulted a number of professionals with backgrounds in medicine, science, and, of course, psychotherapy to convince me I had nothing to be concerned about.

Do I think that all of these irrational fears happened to develop at transitional stages of my life, perhaps to provide a means to cope with the changes? Possibly. Irrational fears—over being electrocuted, swallowing my uvula, or contracting HIV when I wasn't sexually active or an intravenous drug user—served as a distraction from facing the real challenges in my life. This pattern of avoidance would continue into my adulthood.

More importantly, the types of compulsions and fears to which I was prone always seemed to focus on the body. This explains my first truly debilitating problem from OCD: a paralyzing fear of contamination. I was afraid that my body would become contaminated through contact with another person and terrified that I was the tainted one who would contaminate someone else.

In my teenage years, irrational fears over contamination and physical illness complicated the common stresses that most kids my age were already dealing with, like fitting in. Swimming among the sharks and not getting swallowed whole by the social factions and academic cliques at school set the stage for my anxiety and compulsions to breed and multiply.

CHAPTER 1

Bovines in Distress

Part I

I grew up in a small college town in New Jersey. Practically everyone who lived there had a family member or knew someone well who worked at the college. The majority of kids I went to school with were the children of college faculty and staff. And this is not to say that every student who walked the halls of the town's public school system qualified for Mensa and would go on to win MacArthur Genius Grants, but I did sit at the lunch tables in the cafeteria amongst an impressive pool of academic talent.

In middle and high school, I was accepted into honors classes in the humanities and arts but struggled to keep my head above water in math and science. I spent my mornings participating in spirited debates analyzing the themes and symbolism of Kafka and Dante's *Inferno*. In the afternoons, I languished from the effects of isolation and the repetition of equations being beaten into my brain.

I was not a small town girl who enjoyed living where everybody knew everyone else's business. My stepmother had an apartment in Manhattan, and so in my teenage years I grew accustomed to spending weekends in the city. I dreaded returning to New Jersey on Sunday nights to reenter that small town existence. I wanted to escape the banality of life in New Jersey and the academic pressures of a mainstream high school experience. I asked (actually, begged) to go to private school, somewhere perhaps with a more innovative pedagogical philosophy where I could craft my own curriculum.

My father insisted that any private education be integrated with Jewish studies. Because I didn't speak, read, or write Hebrew, attending a Jewish Day School program and studying tenth-grade English and beginner Hebrew would have ostracized me even further. In the end, he said that if I wanted a less traditional high school experience, he would compromise and send me to an American-accredited high school program in Israel. There I could learn Hebrew at my own pace with other beginners and continue my other studies on grade level. My stepmother had also just given birth to twins, so leaving the country and freeing myself from the sounds of two infants wailing at all hours was well timed.

Happily, the culture shock I experienced in Israel was minimal. The students who attended the program came from all over the United States, South Africa, Canada, and the United Kingdom. In addition to our program, there were also Israeli day students that attended class on campus, and Russian boarding students. All of our courses were taught in English, except for Hebrew language studies, and everyone in the program had a different mastery level. Some of my classmates spoke Hebrew at home with their Israeli-born parents; others like me didn't know their Aleph Bet (ABCs). One aspect I quite enjoyed was the siesta, the time of day that everything shut down for an hour so everyone could rest. That was the good part; the bad part was that we had to go to classes on Sundays.

I shared a room with three other girls, one of whom I met before I boarded the plane at JFK. We became fast friends. Twenty-four years later, she remains one of my closest confidantes.

The four of us, my roommates and I, were responsible for keeping up our room and had to pass a dorm inspection before we were permitted to leave campus grounds. That's how I became accustomed to using a squeegee, that cleaning tool with the flat, smooth rubber blade. As we cleaned the bathroom, it functioned as some sort of a hybrid dustpan-mop, sopping up and sweeping the excess water, dirt, and clumps of hair that regularly spilled out of the stall where we showered back down the drain. Today, I tremble at the thought of stepping out of the shower into a tepid, discolored pool of backed-up water. But at the time, it didn't faze me.

Thin sheets and scratchy blankets were provided to us by the school. Once a week, these sheets and blankets, along with my clothing, underwear, and towels, were thrown into the school laundry with large batches of my classmates' clothing, underwear, thin sheets, and scratchy blankets. I'm sure if I'd gone in protest to speak with the brash Israeli women working in the laundry—and expressed any aversion to having my personal items washed with fellow campus residents' in harsh detergents and whitened with bleach containing chemical agents that twenty plus years later have probably been banned in most parts of the world—they would have bristled at my American privilege, chastised my spoiled, insolent attitude, and sent me away with my head down in shame. So it's a good thing it never occurred to me.

Our Middle Eastern studies curriculum included travel to historical locations. Getting to those places required hiking—a lot of hiking. If you moaned and whined about feeling the effects of heat stroke from the oppressive temperatures or refused to wade through tunnels of muck and grime up to your waist, they would threaten to leave you there. This philosophy was used to build endurance. Tough love. And it worked for me! I became less focused on the fetid smells of sewage that would, under any other circumstances, have caused me to retch. Climbing to the top of Mount Masada, I persevered with my wobbly knees and light-headedness, seeking out encouragement from my new friends as well as a little praise and a pat on the head from the staff recognizing a job well done.

Perhaps the experience most effective in suppressing my fears was initiation. All of us had heard about initiation, but as far we were concerned, it was all rumors. It was rumored that a group of graduating seniors would, when we least expected it, bang on the front gate of our dormitory building. This gate was locked and chained at night after we all returned to our rooms for curfew so that the more unruly among us couldn't sneak their way off school property. Then, as the rumor went, they would shout at us in a combination of English and Hebrew, commanding that we wake up from our groggy state, get dressed, and meet them outside. Theoretically, Dan, our *madrich* (youth counselor or program supervisor), would be given a heads up from the seniors and would be on hand to unlock the gates and provide any additional rousing if needed.

We had been told that once we assembled outside, the seniors would separate us. The girls in our group would go with the senior girls, the boys with the senior boys. Then we would perform a number of military-style drills while running across campus.

Our American program was housed on the grounds of an agricultural high school. All students who attended learned to garden, pick grapefruits in the orchards, and work with the animals, and one of the animals students received instruction in how to care for were cows. It was rumored our night would end with a crash course in working with this particular animal.

A few days into the start of the fall semester, shortly after curfew, just as everyone in the dorm was drifting off to sleep, we were shaken by the sounds of rattling chains, banging, and shouting in Hebrew. We heard Dan pull the chain off the gate and begin to make the rounds, checking to see that everyone was out of bed and getting dressed. He knocked on our door and peered his head in to give us a sinister, wry smile. He looked like Jack Nicholson in *The Shining*, sans axe.

Dan was an ardent listener of the Grateful Dead. I think he was too young to have been at Woodstock, but his lifestyle was embedded in the culture. He had a degree in social work, and his career trajectory had included a stint as a counselor at a psychiatric hospital. Dan loved "molding" the kids who came through our program, especially the most troubled ones. Pushing us out of our comfort zones, making us sweat, cry, and bleed—he believed we evolved as better human beings in the process. Watching us be ripped from those comfort zones during initiation was certainly no exception.

"Lets go, guys!" Dan bellowed out in his gravely voice. "Outside in two minutes."

Exactly two minutes later, everyone began assembling outside. Because I was in a hurry, I grabbed the pair of sneakers closest to my bed: my blue Puma suedes. Not counting my hunter green Converse All Stars, those shoes were my favorite. Next to my hiking boots, they also offered the best traction.

For the next thirty minutes, we ran an obstacle course around campus. The seniors leading our group poked us with sticks and ordered us to repeat the drills they yelled as we panted and wheezed. While we ran, the faint sound of bovines in distress grew louder. The heavy, humid, late-summer air hung over us. So did the stench of manure. The smell, growing stronger, began to burn and sting our eyes.

When we reached the cowshed, the seniors commanded us to stop. They circled around us, tapping their sticks against their thighs and the palms of their hands. Berating and belittling us as we winced in pain and disgust (some of us fighting back the urge to dry heave all over them), they ordered us to get in the shed. A few of us choked back tears in defeat; others leaned up against the gate to keep themselves from collapsing and falling in.

One by one, each of us made our way into the pen. The sound of our gagging and screaming drowned out the sounds of sneakers squishing and bodies sinking deeper into mounds of cow dung. We waded out a little farther until we were up to our chests in animal feces. Then they commanded us to stop. We stopped, struggling not to lose our footing.

"Congratulations! You have completed initiation."

Today, I would be planning my obituary, cause of death: E-coli poisoning. But at the time, I was living a vindicating moment of camaraderie. My peers and I had survived initiation, and together, we would spend the next several days applying perfumes, colognes, and body washes to remove the smell of cow shit that had seeped into us. My biggest regret was wearing the blue Puma suedes, which were now ruined. I would have to beg and plead to convince my father to ship a new pair to me.

Part II

While away at school in Israel, I often felt like a bovine in distress. Out of place, a stranger in a strange land, with only rudimentary comprehension of the Hebrew language, I might as well have spent my afternoons out to pasture chewing cud and swatting flies off my tail. Sometimes the feelings of displacement I experienced really weren't that much of a stretch from that of a cow being gawked at by humans passing by.

My odd existence away from the familiar staples of American life made me envious of the simple routines these animals led. At the end of the day, when night fell, they could easily retire from the tall grass outside to the barn or the cowshed. Without a care in the world, these bovine creatures could take comfort in the fact that shelter from rain, wind, and extreme temperatures would always be just a few feet away.

During my time in Israel, I learned a lesson that I carried with me for the next few years. And it was a lesson that served me well: one should never take home for granted. The program I attended was designed to offer participants the opportunity to spend every other Shabbat (day of rest) at the school. Special programming was scheduled that provided the chance for our group to bond, play board games, talk, and get to know each other and the staff of the program in a more intimate way. I cherished these forty-eight hours of singing, lighting candles, group discussions, and catching up on sleep.

Alternate weekends, however, required all of us to leave the school grounds. On Friday afternoons after room inspection until Sunday mornings when classes resumed, we departed by bus or taxi to spend Shabbat with someone on a list of approved relatives, friends, and acquaintances our parents had submitted to the program administrators before we arrived. These alternate weekends offered a great way for program participants to visit with family they might not otherwise get to see on a regular basis. For those of us like me, who had a very short list of family and friends to stay with, our program principal did her best to match us with host families in the area.

In my host family, I had a surrogate mom, dad, three sisters, and a menagerie of animals that were confined to the back-yard and appeared to be slightly emaciated and suffering from mange. At first, spending Shabbat with my host family was great. All of them, except the youngest who was only three, had spent time in America and were either fluent or spoke English well. My adopted mother was kind, soft-spoken, and doted on me. She went out of her way to make sure I felt comfortable when I was staying with them. And my sisters, one of whom was a day student at the high school I attended, invited me to the movies or the beach with them when they went out with their friends.

But soon, my adopted mom, tired of always being responsible for feeding my sisters and me, got frustrated. I think she also felt it would be rude not to speak English around me. My adopted father, who had a gruff exterior and only reluctantly spoke English at all, definitely had also grown weary of my presence in their home.

I began to dread the time in the week when Dan would make his rounds through the dorm with a clipboard to record our weekend plans. I would stammer and try to stall him, saying I hadn't quite gotten everything figured out, but that I would get back to him soon.

"Okay," Dan would sigh, stroking his beard and giving me a piercing look. "Let me know when you've got it all figured out."

The next few hours would be spent on the phone in a heightened state of anxiety, dialing the numbers of everyone on my list, hoping they might be willing to take me in so I could saunter up to Dan and exclaim boastfully that I'd be spending Shabbos with the Rosens or Sterns or whoever else would be kind enough to offer me shelter that week.

Holidays were even more anxiety provoking. Passover was eight days. *Eight days!* Who the hell would be nice enough to open up their home to me for eight days?

With moderate success, I was able to coerce some of my dorm mates to let me tag along with them to Eilat. Picture Daytona Beach at spring break—that was Eilat during Passover, overrun with tourists and reckless teenagers.

My group loved me. They loved my fun-loving spirit, the poem I wrote about having menstrual cramps that I recited in class and submitted to the yearbook, and they loved to watch me stuff my face with falafel. But what they didn't love was spending eight days with a neurotic person when all they wanted to do was camp on the beach and perfect their technique of building bongs out of plastic soda bottles. To them,

I was a group mascot, not someone you wanted to go on an extended vacation with.

When summer came around, I went back to the States. While I was away, my father had decided that because of the rigors of math and science in a mainstream high school program, my best chance of graduating would be to stay abroad and spend my senior year in the same program. In the fall of 1994, I returned to Israel to complete my senior year abroad.

The program was designed to be for one year; only in special circumstances did kids stay on to complete another. This new group of students didn't include my closest friends and roommates, but did include being asked to participate in all the same activities. It included researching and writing another dissertation. I had to do it all over again, and more, without the support and encouragement of those who had already experienced it with me the first time around. I was forced to reinvent myself amongst a completely new and different group of students.

That year, I completed the minimal math and science requirements through one-on-one instruction with a private tutor, who I think had at some point studied geology or maybe archeology. I made a few friends but struggled to find my place within the new group. We didn't have a prom, and weren't taught driver's education.

In the spring of 1995, I finished high school. I won the English Award for the second year in a row but left without submitting even one college application essay. The program facilitators made arrangements for me to take my SATs, untimed, which was permitted in my IEP (Individualized Education Program), but it was really up to the parents to notify the staff of what kind of college preparation they wanted for their children.

Other than taking the required SATs, my father did not issue any instructions. There was no plan for me or my future except to come back home, work part-time, and enroll in a handful of courses at the local community college.

My friends from my former high school had now gone off to start their freshman years. Friends I made abroad would all now scatter too. They would go on to pursue degrees in higher education, enter the Israeli army, travel, or start families. But they all had a plan, or had been offered a foundation to build upon, while the only certainty I knew was that I would soon have no choice but to reinvent myself again.

Much of what happened that following year I've blocked out as a survival mechanism. Within days of being back in the States, I developed what I thought was a rash. It started with a few small patches around the back of my hands and legs, but after a week, it spread to my back, abdomen, and neck. The urge to scratch was excruciating, especially during the night hours when the humidity of summer made falling and staying asleep challenging.

I reported the symptoms to my father. I told him I felt like there were parasites crawling on my body.

While I had been away for two years, my father, induced by his wife, had focused most of his resources, monetary and emotional, on his young twins, and thus essentially had forgotten his other two daughters. My older sister stayed with my mother after the divorce, but my father had been given sole custody of me seven years before. That man did not call in artillery of experts, like he would have when I was a child. He did not hug me and say, "I'm sorry that you don't feel well," or give me a condescending pat on the head. Rather, he said, "It's all in your head, just forget about it."

I tried for well over a month to *just forget about it*. I questioned my sanity over that rash, which consisted of plainly visible blotches. It was painful, and now covered every square inch of my body. For over a month, I suffered in silence.

I was finally permitted to take the New Jersey Transit train into Penn Station to go see my dermatologist. With a cursory look at my hands and back, he grimaced. He backed away from me to scrawl a quick note on his prescription pad, and placed the prescription next to me on the examining table.

"You have scabies. Apply this cream to the affected areas twice a day, and you'll be fine."

Wasn't that a sexually transmitted disease? I wasn't sexually active, so how did I get it? I had questions, but my dermatologist had already fled from the examination room like an Eastern European Jew from the pogroms. I thought he did not want to know how I had contracted this highly communicable condition. I would have to figure that out myself.

When I got home and reported the dermatologist's findings, my stepmother gasped and told me to strip my bed. Then I washed all my linens and towels in boiling-hot water. She essentially quarantined me from the twins and everyone else in the household until I was no longer contagious. It took about a week for my skin to clear, but it was one of the longest weeks of my life.

My mother had also remarried, and had been living in Vermont with my stepfather, who was a tenured professor at the University of Vermont. For almost eight years, unless you count our strained intermittent dinners together, we had virtually no contact with each other. This was in part what I wanted, but also partially because my father and stepmother had been successful in turning me against her.

It took my father's dismissal of my scabies and his abrupt transformation from someone I knew into someone I hardly recognized anymore to reunite us. With the help of my grandmother and mother, I got out of the house and my attic bedroom, wrote an essay, and presented academic transcripts that were good enough to get me accepted to college. I would be reinventing myself again, but this time with the attainable goal of leaving my feelings of displacement behind.

CHAPTER 2

A Moving Story

In the summer of 2013, I moved, and it almost killed me. I only moved six blocks, but those six blocks felt like the distance between Brooklyn and the equator.

I had just completed a nine-month documentary arts fellowship while working full-time and balancing the responsibilities of scheduled production shoots, master class sessions with visiting guest artists, and grappling with making sense of film theory through assigned readings. With both graduate school and then the fellowship, I was on a perpetual hamster wheel, preserving every last ounce of energy to absorb the barrage of material thrown at me. This often led to prolonged feelings of panic that I couldn't quell no matter how much I told myself that everything would be fine. *You held down a full-time job and got a promotion while in graduate school, for Christ's sake. You can handle this, no problem.*

But these preoccupations allowed me to achieve an important goal: they left little to no time for personal reflection, an exercise in concentration and self-discipline that terrified me far more than any Roland Barthes or Walter Benjamin reading.

Because each project bled into the next, they served as perfect distractions from delving into any intense, critical self-analysis. That's probably why I applied to the fellowship at Doc-space only a year after receiving my masters. Devoid of the frenetic pace of juggling multiple ventures, life left a stagnant sensation in the pit of my soul. Still, the excuse of not having to do any work on myself drew me in.

So, I decided, as earning my master's and co-producing documentary shorts satisfactorily covered professional growth, the next logical step seemed to be tackling personal growth. For me, that meant moving from a studio to a one-bedroom apartment. In my mind, I equated adding a door between the living room and bedroom as personal growth, and I had to act quickly in order to avoid deeper self-reflection. I needed to distract myself from slipping into old, dangerous patterns of checking, indulging in irrational thoughts, and other obsessive behaviors.

At first, planning for the move went fine. I was elated over the prospect of a new beginning, taking a risk, and investing more money into making a home that could be permanent, rather than the current one, which I viewed as transient.

Then I started researching moving preparations. Because I lived in New York, a populous, dirty urban hub, it was my natural inclination to research how to protect myself in a move. The literature ran the gamut, from making sure that the moving company was insured to making sure your things were packed securely. But then, of course, there was the section on protecting your property from damage: water, mildew, dust and debris, and bedbugs. If I were smarter, this is where I would have ended my research.

But with each passing day of combing through manuals and Internet surfing, my morning routine and commute to work got longer. Even though I wasn't paying for gas, I tapped the burners on the kitchen stove three, four, five, as many at eight consecutive times to convince myself they were shut off. While I was hunched over the burner, tapping, patting, and stroking the gas range for signs of imaginary heat stoking what I believed would result in a five-alarm fire, I opened and shut the refrigerator and freezer door, feeling around the vent of the unit for escaped pockets of air. I checked to make sure the temperature setting on the thermometer hadn't moved from "freezing" to "quick freeze" or "too warm." I became trapped in a cycle of intrusive thoughts and *what if* scenarios that I couldn't claw my way out of.

What if the bag of expired, freezer-burned Birdseye broccoli, the only item (other than the thermometer) being stored in the freezer, wasn't kept cold enough? Then I would need to buy another bag to replace it and throw it out before the move. What if the three-prong plug on the extension cord connecting the air conditioner and TV brushed up against the grates of the radiator? A quick spark from the plug would only moments later engulf the entire building in flames, leaving me and the other the tenants displaced.

And really, the fellowship hadn't gone well. The timing was perfect, but the experience was not a good fit for my skill set. I was the only participant who worked full-time at a desk job instead of as a freelance media artist, and I believed I was at a disadvantage because I had opted for pragmatism and structure over a life filled with adventure and uncertainty. I was a strong researcher and writer; I was organized and detail oriented, all good qualifications for producing, but I was not comfortable in my skin as a cinematographer and editor. I negated and self-sabotaged the whole nine months through. I left the program feeling like a failure.

Instead of allowing myself a period of time for grief and self-reflection, I jumped into a new project. Moving is stressful enough to give even your most garden-variety neurotic hand tremors and an unexplained eyelid twitch. For someone who struggles with OCD, however, when you add a new layer of anxiety onto what's already a mountainous pile, the results are catastrophic. For me, it meant spooning with everyday household appliances.

Massaging knobs, buttons, door handles, utility drawers. Rubbing and pinching the accordion ridges along the refrigerator door, surveying for breadcrumbs and vegetable peelings invisible to the naked eye, groping and tugging on the handle of the apartment front door.

It meant walking to the bottom of the building stairwell, pausing for a few beats, then pacing and twirling while examining the lobby carpet fibers for dirt and dust particles. All of this provided temporary relief from accepting and processing the string of failures I had arrived at the conclusion were solely my fault and responsibility.

The more clinical definition for "checking" is compulsive behaviors whose purpose is to reduce stress or distress associated with feelings of uncertainty or doubt over feared consequences—for you or others whom you care about, immediate family, friends, pets, etc. This is not how the exact definition appears in the DSM (Diagnostic and Statistical Manual of Mental Disorders), but it's pretty darn close. Here's my definition: compulsive behavior that distracts people with OCD from recognizing and working through the underlying problem. But it's temporary, so after I crouch down to inspect the carpet fibers, I still have to run up the stairs to my apartment again so I can tug on the front door handle another three, four, seventeen times.

This all also came at a time when I was spiraling into a deep depression. Even receiving a piece of joyous news from a family member was enough to set me off.

"I'm preggo, Jen!" my cousin wrote, as I texted her from the laundromat to wish her a happy New Year.

"Wow, that's awesome!" I replied, as I wept uncontrollably and used the dryer sheets as Kleenex to muffle my sobs. I was a loser, bested by my pregnant twenty-something cousin. She was married and having her first kid, achieving all her life goals, while mine were at a complete standstill.

If I had been smarter, I wouldn't have chosen to go off my meds. Or I wouldn't have gone off them cold, but would have weaned myself off them gradually and contacted my psychiatrist before making this decision. Instead, I willfully chose not to reschedule our last canceled appointment.

By the week of the move, I was experiencing symptoms of withdrawal. I had purchased clean boxes at a sidewalk sale from a woman who had just moved in down the block. The boxes were labeled and filled with books, shoes, and unearthed collections of tchotchkes. I packed them, only to unpack and inspect them with a flashlight for bedbugs and then reinspect each corner and crevice. Though I was satisfied that no pest was hidden away, I threw them all out anyway and bought brand new ones from Staples, then hauled them home in the August heat across three avenues in the oversized laundry grocery cart I lovingly referred to as the bubbe cart, the Yiddish word for grandmother. I was eating only intermittently, drinking even less than that, and was sustained by nothing more than the rapid speech and heart palpitations that kept my system from flatlining completely.

All my emotional stress was also manifesting itself physically through a vast range of skin ailments, dermatitis, folliculitis, and eczema. When I went to see my physician for treatment, she prescribed a topical cream and made her best effort to assure me it was not bedbugs. Yet even with all her years of diagnostic training, I was convinced her assessment had to be wrong, and that mine was most assuredly right. I used the cream she prescribed for about a grand total of two days before I called the office in a panic, begging the staff to tell the doctor that I was experiencing rare side effects of stretch marks, elasticized skin, and loss of skin. These were the ones listed in really small print at the bottom of the medication guide that accompanied the prescription. The ones that require twenty-twenty vision to read. I pleaded with the staff to let my physician know that it was imperative that I discontinue use of the medication immediately.

As if this wasn't enough, I was also experiencing early morning crying jags and full-blown panic attacks daily. I would go to bed at 2 A.M., wake at 4 A.M., walk to the bathroom, flip on the light, and begin scanning my arms, abdomen, knees, thighs, and the bottoms of my feet for welts resembling bedbug bites. Unsure of whether my findings indicated rash, eczema, bug bites, or anything at all, I would glare at my reflection in the bathroom mirror and feel my face becoming flushed, my body tremoring, and my eyes becoming moist. I would begin to sob as I wondered yet again how I was going to make it into work that day. After the crying stopped, I would return to my room, boot up my laptop, locate my music files, select Vivaldi, Bach, Schumann—any classical music tracks I had available—and place them in shuffle mode. Then I would climb back into bed and lie there lifelessly listening to stirring overtures.

In any other situation, I would have felt moved by the pathos of the pieces or entranced by their hypnotic interludes. But instead, I was not soothed, and was nowhere near being able to fall back to sleep. Obediently, I would struggle alone and wait for the light to creep in through the window, which signaled that it was now an acceptable hour to call my mother and desperately attempt to receive consolation from her.

At first, my mother demonstrated genuine maternal concern and patience, delaying her run in the park to take our family dog, Lucky, out to pee. Instead, she would listen to me flounder through intervals of convulsing and sobbing to coherent sentences. But it wasn't long before her patience wore thin.

One night, after returning home from work to find a water bug the size of a small sewer rat scurrying across the floor, I called her in hysterics, screaming that I had made a big mistake signing the lease on the new apartment. I would have been much better off if I had just accepted that as much as I wanted to move and start a new chapter in my life, I would never be able to do it.

My mother shouted words that terrified me infinitely more than any common household insect ever could.

"I'm sorry! It's my fault. I never should have made you move, but I can't take this anymore. You have to stop calling me!"

Even my own mother of thirty-six years was giving up on me. I was at my breaking point and needed to get it together or I would risk losing not only my mother, but everyone important to me in my life. I had no choice but to go forward.

So I concentrated on my efforts to regain control and stabilize my mental health. With my therapist, I worked to create a plan to determine, once I was in the new apartment, how many of the sealed, untouched boxes stacked in the hallway I would agree to unpack before our next one, two, or maybe three sessions. Then I met with new psychiatrists.

I instantly hit it off with one, an empathic and innovative thinker, but he didn't accept my health insurance. My therapist also didn't accept insurance, and I couldn't afford to see two out-of-network doctors. Left with no other options, I traded out-of-the-box thinking and a gentle bedside manner for someone highly regarded who was in network, but completely lacking in bedside manner.

Even though I was working to improve my mind-set and embrace the excitement of moving, even though I told myself that moving would be great, to just think of all the new things I would be able to buy to decorate my new home—curtains for the living room and bedroom, towels and a shower curtain for the bathroom—there was only so much my therapist, psychiatrist, and I could accomplish in such a short period of time.

The night before my move, I walked into a Subway sandwich shop on Flatbush Avenue five minutes before closing time. I almost drove the guy behind the counter to drink as he prepared my meager six-inch sub. Every time I waivered about whether I wanted sweet peppers and cucumbers, or maybe just pickles, his temples throbbed and his gaze shifted towards the courtesy cup he was using to swipe soda from the fountain. I envisioned him sneaking a concealed flask out from under the glass counter and pouring whiskey into the cup every time I said, "Actually, I changed my mind: no cheese, just the turkey."

My friend Ruth, a solid, no-nonsense lawyer and single mother of a two-year-old daughter, had offered to help supervise the move. When I arrived home and began to peel the turkey and sweet peppers, which I never actually intended to eat, off my sandwich, I dialed her number.

In a cracked, faltering voice, I announced that I would understand if she did not want to help with my move because I was having an episode and was acting crazy.

Ruth chuckled lightly and retorted, "We'll see how crazy you really are!"

By the time the movers and Ruth arrived the next morning, I'd wrapped the antique children's rocker, which my mother had given me when I first moved to New York, in more than seven layers of plastic. This was to shield it from debris and vermin, though it could just as easily have been wrapped in a quilted moving blanket. I'd only emptied out half of the closet.

I had compartmentalized everything that I wanted the movers to take into two separate corners. In one corner was my furniture, which consisted of a full-size bed, a small reclaimed wood bistro table, three vintage Bentwood chairs, one with a cane seat and two without, a rolling desk, two floor lamps, my love seat, a TV stand, a flat-screen Samsung television, and a microwave. In the other corner were non-furniture items: four boxes of books, three boxes of dishes, miscellaneous kitchen supplies, and a few other assorted keepsakes. That was it!

I told the movers that in no uncertain terms were they to remove my clothing, bedding, toiletries, shoes, or any of the personal financial documents in manila folders that I was unable to fit into packing boxes. I was essentially paying movers not to move anything except the heaviest, most cumbersome items that I owned. In spite of being forced to deal with my harried state, it was the easiest job they'd had all day, possibly all year.

Ruth did not flinch as the two of us haplessly attempted to safeguard my love seat in the plastic sofa cover I had purchased from Home Depot that was at least three sizes too small.

"We can wrap that in a blanket for you," said the head mover as he watched this bewildering display unfold before him.

"No!" I said, alarmed. Then I smiled, trying furiously to mask my unraveling composure.

"No," Ruth replied emphatically. She was doing her best to communicate to the head mover how urgent it was for him to comply with my request. She eyed him squarely and firmly. "We'll use the plastic cover instead."

"Okay." The head mover shrugged and motioned to his crew to stand down and refrain from touching anything containing upholstery or fabric.

He had left a set of written instructions from his boss and dispatcher lying on my desk. I caught a glimpse of them while he and the other movers were busy working. At the bottom, in bold caps, the instructions read, "YELP REVIEW JOB MUST BE PERFECT."

After calling the company twice in the past week, I had come very close to going with another mover and canceling them altogether. Clearly, they were under strict orders to heed and respect all of the troublemaking client's requests. It didn't matter how bizarre, unhinged, or monetarily wasteful those requests might be.

I had scheduled the move into the new apartment a week before the lease on the current one was set to expire. I intended to move all my clothes, personal papers, and tchotchkes piece-meal and on my own throughout the course of the week. In hindsight, being responsible for the upkeep of two apartments simultaneously probably wasn't the best decision. My landlord's assistant called and emailed several times trying to get me to commit to a firm move-out date so they could paint the apartment. But I refused to divulge any specifics other than I would be out before midnight on the day the lease ran out. This made them irate, but I didn't care. I knew how difficult it would be to estimate the number of trips I would need to make with the bubbe cart between the old apartment and the new one. I wasn't about to shortchange myself, even if it had the potential to alleviate a hefty portion of the stress I was experiencing.

The move itself went well. Nothing was broken or torn. The glass plate from my microwave went missing, but other than that, it was a fairly seamless process. Ruth and I removed the many layers of plastic wrap from the rocker and rearranged the furniture in the bedroom. I took out a flashlight to inspect between the grooves of the mattress for any unseemly crea-tures that might be lurking. We tossed out the love seat cover, used in lieu of moving blankets, and positioned the sofa a few feet away from the TV and TV stand, which the movers had assembled before leaving for their next job.

Now that they were gone, and the furniture temporarily arranged, I was starting to feel more at ease. My mother, who already had a set of keys, had visited the apartment a handful of times to measure and hang curtains in the living room and bedroom. She also arranged to have her cleaning lady clean the apartment before the move. Thus every surface of the 650-square-foot space had been scoured and scrubbed in time for the first night in my new home.

Paying to have the apartment cleaned prior to the move was an incredibly warm and generous gesture on her part. It was perhaps also an extended olive branch. My mother felt responsible for my struggles because she had goaded me to move. She was unabashedly delighted when I told her about my decision. Sure, she had made me more conscious of the stained carpeting in the downstairs foyer of the brownstone building I had called home for the past three years, but it was a decision I would have made regardless. If I hadn't moved, the struggles I experienced with common, daily tasks, like getting out of bed and going to work—or sitting on my sofa in clothes that had been worn outside instead of stripping down to my underwear the second I walked in the door and stuffing the clothes into garbage bags until they could be laundered—would have found other ways to manifest themselves.

The next day, I began transporting everything left behind at the old apartment over to the new one with the bubbe cart. To a bystander, I was quite a sight to see: my hair was matted and weighed down from beads of perspiration as I struggled to wheel the cart filled with sweaters, sneakers, and more than five years of bank statements. I stopped every few blocks to collect stacks of papers that had fallen out of the cart; I wasn't skilled enough to maneuver my way around the cracked and pothole-ridden sidewalks and maze of double-wide strollers lining 7th Avenue, Park Slope's bustling main drag.

I left behind my air conditioner, because union rules only allowed insured moving companies to move them. Installing or uninstalling an AC unit would have been considered a liability. I also believed that there was a clause in my old apartment lease that stated once an air conditioner was installed, it became the property of the landlord; if I didn't leave it behind, I would be violating the lease agreement. I'm not exactly sure how I arrived at this interpretation, but I was certain that if I did not obey it, I would be subject to some type of unthinkable physical torture, like flogging. More importantly, I knew that if I violated the clause my security deposit wouldn't be returned to me.

After the sixth or seventh trip between apartments, I knew that I would not be able to endure this existence much longer. Soon I'd need to enlist the help of someone else, preferably someone with a car.

When I returned to the office on Monday, my friend, coworker, and close confidante, Roxy, asked how the move went. I waffled a little in my response, but ultimately revealed to her that there was still work to be done. It didn't take long for her to figure out I was asking for help. She could tell I was struggling and needed her. Four years earlier, Roxy had helped me pack up the East Midtown rent-controlled apartment I'd lived in for seven and a half years before moving into a more spacious brownstone studio apartment in Brooklyn. She was no-nonsense, just like Ruth, but also knew how to tread lightly when I was in a fragile emotional state.

By the time Roxy and I arranged a meeting date to complete my move, the feeling of relief and ease I had experienced the day of the move had almost disappeared. Instead, I was a disheveled, blubbering mess, belaboring under the delusion that the prickly heat rash lining my arms, neck, and abdomen was the result of bedbugs siphoning my blood during their night feedings.

Roxy held and consoled me as I doused her arm with my tears and used her sleeve as a makeshift handkerchief. When

I finally calmed down, she was gentle. She knew that if we were going accomplish anything, then this was not the time to challenge my irrational fears. It was best to just indulge me, at least for now. Throughout that night, Roxy maintained an organized and efficient manner. She remained focused on the move while I paced back and forth. I wanted desperately to be proactive and work with her, but achieved little more than watching with a glazed look on my face.

She bundled together skirts, winter coats, and dress pants onto hangers and covered them with the same type of Hefty trash bags I had used to protect and transport my bed linens. Under normal circumstances, these bags are used outdoors to gather muck and debris trapped in the rain gutters, or wet, pungent leaves papering the front lawn—not for clothing. For me, they were the only bags I trusted to safeguard any garment that might come in contact with my body from unwanted visitors searching for a point of entry. To this day, many of the clothes that Roxy lovingly gathered that night remain in those black Hefty trash bags, drawstrings still double knotted.

By the time spring arrived, life had begun to resume normalcy. The contents of sealed boxes stacked in the hallway of my apartment were emptied onto shelves and into closets. The boxes were discarded. I compromised with my therapist that in lieu of stuffing clothes worn outside into garbage bags, I would hang them in the front hallway closet.

Multiple trials of psychotropic drugs were experimented with until the right combination was found. So my mood began to stabilize and the anxiety to dissipate. Everything seemed to be going fairly well. I felt noticeably better. It was time once again to ask myself that big, looming question: what was next?

CHAPTER 3

No Eggs, No Cheese, No Milk.
Did I Mention, No Ice?

In late spring of 2014, when I submitted my application to attend an Eco-Explorers ten-day trip to Costa Rica with twelve other young Jewish professionals, I thought I was ready. I had been living in my one-bedroom apartment for almost a year. No calamity of blood, pestilence, famine, or even bedbug infestation had befallen me. I was finally starting to feel comfortable in my new surroundings. So, I figured, why not think big? Neither my therapist nor my psychiatrist vetoed the idea. They were, in fact, quite receptive to it and agreed that I was ready.

When most people think of Costa Rica, they visualize an oasis filled with coral beaches and zip-lining adventures. They don't hear Costa Rica and think rabid bats, venomous snakes, and malaria-infected mosquitoes; they don't bypass fantasizing about beautiful, misty rain clouds to envision E. coli tainted drinking water spouting from the tap. And cholera.

But I did.

I polled and grilled my coworkers who had traveled to regions of the world where taking malaria pills was either required or recommended and asked them to detail any adverse side effects they had experienced. One mentioned something cited on the CDC website (from which I had begun taking copious notes): weird dreams. These weren't the fun hallucinations you get from doing mushrooms, but the kind that makes you feel detached from reality and unaware of your surroundings. It was common, and it could potentially impede my overall experience on the trip.

Once again, I approached Roxy. I paced back and forth in front of her desk, managing to maintain a hint of professionalism—but I still failed to fight back the tears slowly welling up as I debated whether or not it was worth it to cancel the trip and lose the deposit I had already paid on my credit card.

Roxy demonstrated her usual calm exterior. It always left me awestruck. With a company headset plastered to her ear, she waited on hold for the travel service to connect her phone call so she could make modifications to the upcoming trip itinerary, responded verbally to queries from her boss (whose office was less than thirty feet from her desk), and simultaneously typed out a list of pros and cons for me on her laptop. This list laid out why I should go or cancel the vacation.

When Roxy was finished, she read off the list with the soothing intonations I had grown so accustomed to in times of suffering and personal crisis. Reasons to go included: this might very well be a once-in-a-lifetime opportunity. I was in my late thirties and wouldn't have the agility and endurance to slog through the rainforest forever, so better to go now while I still had some semblance of stamina. Another pro was meeting young professionals from all over the country. We had already started bonding over email and Facebook group postings; it would be terrible to give up the chance to get to know them in person. Then, of course, there was my primary motive to go: the possibility that I might meet a nice Jewish boy and enter into a longtime relationship.

The list of reasons not to go included: the possible side effects I might experience if I took malaria pills, and contracting dengue fever, for which no preventative measures could be taken to protect myself from. If I did contract dengue fever, I might only experience minor flu-like symptoms, but in some cases the effects of the illness were dire.

Conflicted about taking malaria pills, I wrestled with how to safeguard myself from disease if, in the end, I decided to forgo treatment, which was the direction I was leaning. A few of my colleagues who had just returned from a production shoot in Costa Rica mentioned that they had used an insecticide called permethrin to treat their clothing. After reviewing a YouTube tutorial, I learned that permethrin had to be applied with a spray and left to air-dry outdoors for a period of several hours.

For me this was problematic on many levels. I lived in New York City in a 650-square-foot apartment. One of my colleagues who had used the spray to treat her clothing lived in the suburbs with a house and a big backyard, so leaving her clothes outside on the clothesline overnight wasn't an issue. What was I supposed to do? Drape my entire wardrobe over the banister leading to the front stoop of my building and hope that no one stole my clothes? Hang them out my bedroom window? How about buying fishing wire, piling all my clothes in the bubbe cart, wheeling everything over to Prospect Park, and tacking the fishing wire to a tree as a makeshift clothesline? That sounded pretty fail-safe. No holes in that master plan at all.

So no, I thought, either I subject myself to insecticide poisoning or cancel the trip. After a brief period of reflection, I recited a list of reasons to Roxy as to why I would cancel the trip. To me, all the reasons seemed reasonable. This, of course, is one of the prime characterizations of OCD: that irrational thoughts always seem rational. And rational ideas can come across as irrational. This is especially true during prolonged periods of heightened stress and anxiety.

Roxy rolled back and forth on the rubber core-strengthening ball she used as a desk chair and listened intently to the stream of hypersensitive nonsense flowing from my mouth. Although Roxy had never had children, she possessed maternal instincts and fortitude, wisdom, and patience like nothing I had ever seen from an actual mother. She had worked as a doula for many years and knew how to navigate through a high-stress situation. She was protective of her friends like a mother bear of her young. You could always count on Roxy.

Not long after I had started working at our company, one of my coworkers arranged for everyone in the office to take a sunset cruise around the city. Once the cruise ended, we would all gather at a nearby watering hole for a quick cocktail. My coworker picked a sports bar that was loud and filled with rowdy twenty-something men who displayed both an affinity for the New York Mets and a desire to mark their territory.

While we were waiting in line to get our IDs checked at the door, one of these men pinched and grabbed my female coworker Sally by the ass. Roxy whipped her head around and smacked the guy right across the face. As he gripped his stinging face in a state of disbelief, Roxy waved her finger and said, "If you touch my friend again, the next ass you'll be grabbing will be of the guy you're sharing a prison cell with."

"Well, Jen-Jen," (this was her nickname for me), "maybe I can help."

Help? How?

"Maybe," she went on, "I can ask my landlord if we can use the front yard of the house and spray your clothes there."

Roxy had recently moved into a two-family house in the Astoria neighborhood of Queens. Her landlord lived in the downstairs part of the house. I knew that asking a favor like that could potentially jeopardize her rapport with the landlord, but Roxy wanted me to go on that trip. It had been a tough year, and she genuinely believed I deserved to go. As always, she was ready to walk a mile over smoldering coals to come to my aid. I vowed to make it clear to her I would do the same when she needed it most.

So I didn't cancel my flight or vacation plans. Instead I went to Target and REI and bought all the breathable, moisture-wicking, lightweight-but-long-sleeved tops I could find in my size. At Target I also bought a twenty-pack of women's athletic tube socks, enough to last for the duration of the trip. From my perspective, the socks were multipurpose; I could use them for hiking expeditions through the mud of the rainforest as well as to effectively cover every bare inch of skin that could potentially be exposed to mosquitoes, venomous snake bites, and scorching rays of sun.

Then I purchased the largest spray bottle of permethrin in stock. And, just to be safe, sought recommendations from store employees for the top DEET-free insect repellants. The day before I was scheduled to depart, also on recommendation, I purchased two packs of lavender dryer sheets. The smell was apparently effective in repelling a mélange of biting and stinging insects usually encountered in areas like Costa Rica. My plan was to stuff them into my jacket and pants pockets to strengthen my odds against the attacks of hungry hosts.

The Saturday before I left, I stuffed the twenty-pack of athletic tube socks, moisture wicking long-sleeved shirts, a pair of REI hiking pants that converted into shorts, and other articles of clothing I anticipated taking with me into an oversized canvas bag. I added the twenty-four-ounce pump spray bottle of Sawyer permethrin and boarded the subway to Roxy's home in Queens.

Roxy picked me up at 5 P.M. across the street from the Astoria Boulevard stop on the Q train. We loaded the supplies and clothing into the trunk of her 1987 chocolate-brown Lincoln Town car, inherited from a close friend, and set off to complete the spraying project we both hoped would successfully bring me "peace of mind."

When we arrived, she gave me a tour of the new apartment and we booted up her company-owned laptop. We loaded the YouTube tutorial and watched intently as we were presented with a step-by-step guide on how to apply and pretreat clothing with Sawyer products.

The narrator, Amy, wore a Sawyer-branded, zippered pull-over shirt. She exhibited a pleasant, breezy manner while an upbeat chorus of banjos played in the background. Despite this, I felt a wave of anxiety building. During the tutorial, with a firm smile, Amy instructed us to apply three ounces of permethrin spray to each article of clothing. As she spoke, I became more nervous. How was one supposed to gauge what three ounces of liquid would look like on a shirt versus a pair of socks? Would the area of one smaller article of clothing saturate more than a larger piece? Amy's approachable style made it all sound so easy . . . but was it?

As benign as the approximation of these metrics might sound, for someone who struggles with OCD, there's a difference between having "peace of mind" and spending ten days of vacation convinced that you are only hours away from contracting dengue fever.

We examined each garment, comparing and contrasting the area Amy covered until we were satisfied that our handiwork matched hers. After the contents of the spray bottle had been emptied, we carefully hung each pretreated item on the fence surrounding the front lawn of the house. While the clothes air-dried, we set out to dinner at an Irish pub,

Dinner out and karaoke were activities Roxy loved to partake in once a month with a group of other sassy women. These three were full of pep and a strong dose of piss and vinegar, they were. Roxy sang with them every Sunday and on holidays at her local church, and they embodied a delicate balance of warmth and comic relief. I was always delighted when I had the opportunity to join them.

After satiating ourselves on burgers, steak fries, and Caesar salads, we drank cocktails mixed with Jack Daniels and ginger ale and belted out an eclectic string of Rogers and Hart, Aretha Franklin, and Beatles ballads. Then I offered to pay for dinner and Roxy, as usual, refused.

At the end of the night, we said our goodbyes and dropped each of the choir ladies, as we affectionately referred to them, at their respective doorsteps. Then we returned to Roxy's to retrieve my pretreated clothing and send me back to Brooklyn, from where I would now be able to leave armed and ready for next Saturday's departure.

I wrapped my arms tightly around Roxy and hugged her, never wanting to let go.

"Thank you, Rox, I love you so much," I said.

"You're welcome, Jen-Jen. You know I'm always here for you. Anything, anytime, anywhere," Roxy replied.

↬

The following Saturday morning, I arrived at Newark Airport confident that I was ready to spend the next two weeks in the coastal Caribbean area of Costa Rica. But there was one other thing I had read about that required protection. I had read that in some areas you needed to be vigilant when consuming drinking water and ice. So I had vowed, in spite of sweltering temperatures, to refrain from consuming tap water. Only bottled water, no ice for me the next two weeks—no exceptions.

So, beginning with the plane ride over, I abstained from the pleasure derived from sucking and chewing those delectable, digestible frozen spheres.

"Why not enjoy ice now while you can?" asked the steward.

"Might as well start getting used to it."

The family man of three who was sitting in the aisle seat furrowed his brow with regret for having been assigned to sit next to me. As the hours passed, I described my permethrin-treated clothing, travel insurance, travel health insurance, vaccinations, and the assortment of 30% DEET, 90% DEET, and DEET-free repellants divided into TSA-approved liquid sizes in my carry on and my checked baggage. From his expression, I could see he felt ill prepared to protect his family from disease, sun exposure, and missed flight connections. Though in the event that his family did become stranded, he could take comfort in the fact that he had remembered to pack every iPhone, iPod, and iPad in the house and several jumbo-size variety packs of licorice and gummy candies.

We landed safely and made our way from the airport. After checking into our hotel in San José, Tour Guide Avi escorted five other travelers and me to a local family-owned lunch counter a few blocks from the hotel. He proudly sauntered up to the window to place our orders, suggesting that we all try the tamarind juice. I took temporary solace in hearing the resounding demand of "No ice!" simultaneously barked at him.

"Really?" Avi said, his voice waning and his body dejected. "The water here is safe. I drink right out of the tap."

Weary but content, I sipped my tamarind juice and surveyed the room: a dripping sink in the open kitchen, food scraps on the floor, utensils wrapped in plastic. Everyone in the restaurant had ice in their drinks except for me and the other five Americans sitting at our table. Kindred spirits, I thought to myself.

We were only a few days into the trip before a host of abdominal issues attacked Big Joe, then Little Joe, then Ben. My strategy in response to Patient Zero and the other victims was to scale back on eating an already short list of approved food and drink. With each heave, hurl, and sight of jaundiced skin, no ice became no eggs, no cheese, no milk, and certainly no tap water, not even for brushing teeth. When a collapsible cup and bottled water weren't available, my finger and dry brushing were a satisfactory substitute.

In spite of the heat, I was also remaining committed to my first rule: no short sleeves. This was enforced to protect me from multiple species of mosquitoes, spiders, army ants, bullet ants, and vampire bats. While the rabies vaccine was recommended by some sources, this primarily pertained to travelers intending to come in direct contact with animals. But it was easy enough to get scratched, licked, or jumped on. Even though it pained me deeply, I didn't pet the dogs that trotted up to me at rest stops while I waited in a line for the bathroom or to purchase bottled water. No matter how much I longed to, I was not going to cave. I would not allow a cute wag of the tail to entice me. I held steadfast, refusing the urge to take their paw each time it was offered.

When the group visited an animal rescue center, I posed with a baby doe for a picture and allowed it to chew on the drawstring of my jacket. This was my best attempt to distract it from licking my hand and exposing me to what I believed could be infected saliva. I felt comfortable with my decision until my trip mate Eve berated me, yelling, "Careful! The baby could choke!"

For ten days, I endured oppressive temperatures, poolside Piña Coladas, and introductions to new and exotic fruits. I resisted all temptation and was determined to stick to my rules. But an adventurous spirit will always rise up. Three days before our return to the states, we arrived in Arenal for our zip line tour through the jungle canopies. At this point, I had bonded with my fellow travelers, most of whom were younger and more agile than I. When Big Joe, Little Joe, and Ben became ill from what probably was travel diarrhea, and a few others became progressively more nauseous and weak from the unrelenting heat, I swooped in with the "International Traveler's Kit" I'd received after my travel vaccinations, a free service offered by my company. The kit contained an assortment of emergency medical supplies: gauze, a pair of scissors, iodine, antiseptic cleansers, surgical gloves, cold tablets, and most importantly, pills for extreme nausea and travel diarrhea.

I swore up and down to the group that I had not gone out on my own to purchase these supplies, that they had been provided free of charge through my company. But the skepticism communicated through their raised brows and snickering was palpable. In the end, though, they were appreciative of my over-preparedness, and I had to give pause and wonder if Doctors Without Borders was as well equipped as I.

In the hour leading up to the bus that would take us to Arenal's premiere zip line adventure center, I pulled on my convertible hiking pants, one of the moisture-wicking long-sleeved shirts, and switched to my old pair of glasses; I wouldn't care if they got damaged or fell off as I was suspended in midair. I then swallowed an Ativan. It was the first one I had taken the whole trip, but I was hard-pressed to think of a scenario where consuming a controlled substance would be more beneficial.

When we arrived, the guides assigned to our tour took us to an equipment closet where we chose helmets and gloves. Then they provided a safety overview, had us sign a waiver releasing them of any liability in the event the cable should snap and we plummet to our death, and piled us into the flatbed of a truck that would take us to the starting platform of our adventure.

When we arrived to the first platform, I stood at the back of the line—*way* at the back of the line. Then I watched as my trip mates squealed in delight over the adrenaline rush and feelings of exhilaration. When it came to my turn, I clutched the pulley with a death grip. My hands were sweating so profusely that the perspiration penetrated through my gloves. I was sure that the suspension cable would never be able hold me and regretted not making out my last will and testament prior to departure.

Each platform leading into the next grew with intensity and challenge. So did my terror. At the halfway point, I asked, "How much longer is this going to take?" Instead of squealing with delight, I was screaming in horror.

I told the guides and Avi that I didn't think I could go on any longer and that I was going into full panic mode. The three burly men grimaced and told me that if I wanted to go back on the truck then I had to do it now. Once we arrived at the next platform on the course, there would be no going back until it was over.

Pensively, I circled the platform a few times as I considered my plight. *No going back until it was over?*

I tugged on my chin, bit down on my lip, groaned, grimaced, and contorted my facial muscles into every imaginable position. *What were the chances I wouldn't be going back at all?* I looked over at my trip mates; what it must be like to go through life so bold, so daring, so incomprehensibly stupid?

They began to cheer me on. "Don't give up now, Jen! We won't let anything happen to you, Jen!" I paused for a moment, took a deep sigh, gripped the pulley cable, positioned myself on the platform, and cried out defiantly, "Okay, fine, but all of you better be at my funeral to give a damn good eulogy."

Instead of enjoying the majestic views of capuchin, howler, and spider monkeys swinging from the canopies of the trees, I screamed, hyperventilated, winced, whimpered, and kept my eyes closed for almost the entire time. I only allowed them to open for a fleeting moment when I would need to position myself for a safe landing onto the next platform.

Then it was all over. My trip mates cheered and hugged me, and I waited for my breath to return to normal and for my leg tremors and heart palpitations to subside.

In the end, I would not need to use my travelers insurance. I did not need to plead to be medevaced home. Roxy was right. And I safely made it back to the airport with my friends, posed for some photos to be shared on Facebook, hugged them goodbye, and promised to email them soon.

When I boarded the plane, I was flooded with a wave of mixed emotions over leaving my new friends and returning to my home life. I was also proud.

After we took off, the flight attendant came down to take our drink orders. I figured since I was still on vacation, I may as well indulge myself and order a coke. I leaned back in my seat as the attendant rustled through the drawers in her cart and popped the top on the can. At the sound of the pop, I sat up and cried out in anguish, "Wait! No ice!"

CHAPTER 4

I Hope I Didn't Lose You

The "Pop Culture Happy Hour" podcast on NPR arbitrarily landed on my playlist one early October evening. I had never heard the show before, but as I listened to their thoughtful analysis of *Gilligan's Island*, my dark mood lightened and I found myself transported to an ethereal state far from the despondent mood I had been in—the one that made me feel like whatever course of action I took to regain control of my life, another outside force possessing Herculean strength would, at any moment, swoop down and yank away that control from me.

A more common name for that force is depression. But depression was no match for host Linda Holmes and her team of co-contributors, who seemed to truly delight in the topics they were discussing. As I walked, listening intently, I started to notice the nuances of color in the autumn foliage. Not just red, but a rust-colored red. The crisp fall air had a sweet smell, and the inside of my head didn't feel like it was stuffed with sacks of cotton. I could feel a smile slowly creeping across my face with each cinephile factoid. As they apparently always did, the hosts closed by sharing with their listeners what had made them happy this week. Could their sage knowledge of pop culture be the secret elixir to cure my mental infirmity?

BoJack Horseman was making cohost Glen Weldon happy this week. With a cast he couldn't believe he hadn't thought of himself, he proclaimed the show a must-see. And the first season was streaming on Netflix.

Maybe it was the pure joy in his voice that captivated me, or perhaps it was that someone on public radio was talking passionately about a TV show, but I knew that I had to see it. Amy Sedaris. Will Arnett. Patton Oswalt. Aaron Paul. As each name was read, a magnificent pyrotechnic display set off in my head. When he said, "Aaron Paul," I thought I heard him say, "Stephen Colbert," and something took over my body.

Then Glen began to explain the premise: an animated series about a half-horse, half-man—a washed-up, misanthropic actor from the hit 90s sitcom *Horsin' Around* who hadn't done anything since the show ended its run. He was now trying to reinvent himself by writing his memoir.

I started to glow. I was elated. I would order Chinese and be in for the night. This had the potential to make me feel something that I hadn't felt in a long time . . . happy. When I arrived home, I hurriedly changed into a T-shirt and boxers, positioned myself on the couch, and prepared to have a life-affirming experience.

I waited for the apps on my smart TV to load.

Tonight it seemed to be taking an unusually long time to boot up. I was growing impatient and nervous as I watched the screen continue to buffer. This never happened. Then, suddenly, the buffering icon disappeared, replaced by a small message: "Error. You are not connected to the Internet. Please check your settings and try again."

Calmly, I walked over to the TV to check the cables and the signal on the wireless router. Noting that everything appeared fine, I went into the bedroom to test my laptop. The same taunting message popped up instantly: "Error. You are not connected to the Internet. Please check your settings and try again."

I took a deep breath and began to slowly rub my fingers across my forehead, back and forth in a meditative, circular motion as I thought about what to do next. I shuffled back into the living room, gently unplugged the router, and waited a few seconds before plugging it back in again. That would work. It always worked.

One green light flickered for a few moments, then the next, each one slowly returning to life.

"This will work," I repeated to myself. "This will work."

It had to work. I was sure of it. I needed to believe that everything would be okay.

"Error. You are not connected to the Internet. Please check your settings and try again."

I now had a choice: admit defeat or change strategy. Defeat was not an option. As much as it pained me to do so, it was time to make a call. Swallowing hard, I picked up my cell phone, keyed in the number for Time Warner Cable, and waited patiently.

When my call was finally picked up, I was routed to an automated technical assistant who provided me with the troubleshooting steps I had already taken on my own. I continued to rub my temples, muttering under my breath as I waited for the voice on the other end of the line to finish talking.

When a woman, possibly from the Philippines, answered, I made my case. The hour was growing late, and time was of the essence. No matter what, I was going to at least complete watching the pilot of *BoJack Horseman* sometime between now and when I had to leave for work in the morning.

After about fifteen minutes of troubleshooting, we were able to resolve the issue with the Internet connection on my laptop, but not with the TV. If I had been thinking rationally, it might have occurred to me that I could watch the pilot on my laptop. Regrettably, it did not. Rather, I was convinced that I was doomed to suffer. Besides, should I compromise my preferences by watching on a fifteen-inch screen instead of a forty-two-inch one? Not on your life.

"No," I said, sighing, "that didn't work either—" I stopped talking and realized there was no one on the other end. The call had dropped. I was livid. My body was convulsing. Time Warner, hapless in their efforts as usual, had failed me again. Since it was now well past 11 P.M., I knew that customer service and technical support for Samsung would be closed for the evening. But they did offer a feature for live online chats.

I pulled up the site map on the Samsung website. After several seconds, a live chat with someone who referred to themselves as "Peterson" appeared in the chat window. Ready to assist, they asked that I supply the model number of the product I was using and briefly describe the issue I was having. I entered the information and waited for Peterson to reply.

A lengthy period of time elapsed waiting for Peterson's

response. I began to drum my fingers on the touch pad and sigh heavily.

What felt like several minutes later, a pop-up window indicated that they were typing a response: "You will need a Lync stick for wireless capability."

The blood began to rush to my head. "A Lync stick?" I shrieked to no one in particular. "I've never needed one before!"

Peterson started to type again. "I hope I didn't lose you."

"No," I tapped back, massaging my temples. "Peterson, you didn't lose me. I just need a moment to process this."

Peterson began to type again. "What was the model number of your smart TV?"

I stooped over the back of the TV. "I hope I didn't lose you," Peterson wrote again.

"I'm still here!!!" I typed passionately. The exclamation points were so that Peterson could recognize the direness of the situation.

I typed the serial number out and waited for them to respond.

My cell phone rang. I glanced at the screen. The call was coming from a 1-800 number: Time Warner Cable. My agent was calling me back to say she had spoken with her supervisor, who had told her this was no longer a matter for which Time Warner could provide technical support. I would need to contact Samsung directly for any additional assistance.

"I already did that! I'm online with them right—" I grabbed my laptop. I had been so distracted by the call that I had forgotten about Peterson.

"Okay, well thank you for contacting Time Warner Cable. Have a nice—" but I had already hung up.

Shaking, I read Peterson's response. "That model requires a Lync stick for wireless capability. If you were able to operate the unit without a Lync stick before, then the unit is malfunctioning and will require a technician to review the issue further. Please contact Samsung to schedule service at your earliest convenience."

I proceeded to convey every human emotion I could think of. Frustration, anger, humiliation, and complete desperation. I hoped that the anguish I was feeling would somehow be felt by Peterson through my carefully composed sentences and that Peterson would take pity on me and offer one last suggestion.

Peterson was typing. "There is one other thing we haven't tried yet," they wrote. "We will need to wipe all your current settings on the unit. I need to know that you are okay with this. Can you confirm that you are?"

The urgency in Peterson's words was palpable. I felt like I was being asked to cut off all my limbs. At that point, I would have done it.

"Yes."

Peterson proceeded to send me a PDF document containing instructions on how to "wipe the unit." I studied the document intently, ready to conquer the task at hand. This would work. It had to work. *BoJack Horseman* was still possible. I just had to remain in control.

Despite my meticulous attention to detail and fierce determination, it didn't work.

I took a deep breath and prepared to report my findings to

Peterson. As I glanced down at my computer screen, I felt my lip begin to quiver and wiped a tear from my cheek. "I hope I didn't lose you," the screen said again, but this time the words seemed full of genuine concern.

"No!" I wrote. "That did not work either!"

Peterson wrote back with a hardened tone. "I'm afraid there is nothing else I can do to address your issue."

"Make no sense, why a wireless connection before and not one now!"

"You need a Lync stick for a wireless connection, but you can still access your TV through a wired connection."

A wired connection? "How do I do that?" I asked.

Peterson sent a new document that included an illustration of an LAN network cable, which, if I had one, would be located at the back of the TV. I was sure that I didn't have one because if I did I would have seen it earlier.

I peered behind the TV again. There it was: a mustard-yellow cable identical to the illustration Peterson had sent me.

I unplugged and plugged the cable back into the wall and followed the steps. It took several attempts to get Netflix back in order, but eventually a new message flashed across the screen: "Login Successful."

Ecstatic, I returned to my laptop to inform Peterson of the good news. They had typed another message: "I hope I didn't lose you."

And then several minutes later, "It looks like you are no longer responding or the connection has been lost."

And at the bottom a pop-up window read, "Chat Ended."

"It's okay, Peterson, good buddy. You did your due diligence, got me through a rough patch. Together we persevered, and now, finally, I can watch my show. Maybe we'll meet again someday, don't know how, don't know when. Anyway, Peterson, thank you, for giving new name to the word 'support.' I sincerely hope that whomever you help next doesn't lose you."

Drenched in perspiration, my eyes crusted over from sleeplessness, I sat down and prepared myself to have an enthralling experience. Exhausted, but feeling a little bit wiser and more in control than before.

CHAPTER 5

The Dressing Room

In some way, being alone in a dressing room resembles writing. There's nothing between you and yourself but naked, exposed skin. In either instance, you stand alone, unarmed, ill-equipped to face your life's traumas. In both, people from your past and present taunt you as you try to articulate the words to express your fear, anger, or disdain.

It doesn't help when the sales person calls to you from outside the stall, "How's it going in there? Do you need another size?"

When you respond sheepishly, "Nope, I'm fine," what you really want to say is, "Can't you see I'm busy in here fighting my inner demons?"

The act of trying on clothes is supposed to be a pleasurable experience. It's an opportunity to do something nice for yourself, to splurge and purchase a new outfit to show off at an event or around the office. But for the duration of my adult life, I have dreaded clothes and shoe shopping. I prefer to glare at my doughy, hairy ass cheeks in the reflection of the full-length mirror and spew venomous hate towards my physical appearance.

I don't have a face so hideous that if someone's eyes meet mine they turn to stone. Why can't I embrace myself long enough to see what others see? Or at the very least, put in enough work, as many people do, regardless of gender, to polish my appearance so that they will see me as moderately attractive? Why is it such an alien concept?

When I do finally stop sighing and muttering under my breath long enough to fasten a new bra I'm trying on, I pack my breasts into the cup like I'm storing away moth-eaten clothes in an attic box; I don't place my bosom gently into the cup as I embrace my body and sexuality. I'm pensive, irritable, and anxious to get out of this cold, claustrophobic dressing room, this stale, olfactory nightmare.

If I'm clothes and shoe shopping with friends, my mother, or other relatives, and they have the esteemed pleasure of witnessing me angrily tugging on a shirt, or for some unearthly reason managing to catch a button on a thread and unraveling the fabric, they will shake their head. They gasp, "Why are you being so rough on yourself?" I don't have a plausible explanation for this, but have spent many, many years in therapy trying to make sense of it.

Even the few possessions that I do own become easily battered. It's not that I don't value them. Of course I do. But within only hours of receipt, I'll look down to find a broken zipper, a gaping hole in my shoe, or a spot on a blouse. I'm better off not having anything nice at all, because it will only get ruined instantly.

For example, take the Steve Madden nylon backpack I received as a gift for my birthday this year. Less than a month after I'd gotten it, there were water and ink stains lining the bottom and the zippered pocket on the front had ripped. Five months later, I still refuse to part with it.

The combined amount of time, energy, and money I've put into concealing the rip could have been used to buy five new backpacks. Instead, I've gone through four rolls of electric tape, which I use to cover the opening where the pocket once zippered. I should mention that electric tape is not the most effective adhesive on nylon, so the fact I've used four rolls isn't surprising. Each time I apply the tape, it loses its stickiness, buckles, curls up around the sides, and falls off. I apply a new layer of tape before leaving work for the day, but that falls off usually while I'm in transit. Minutes after boarding the subway, another rider will tap me on the shoulder to state the obvious.

"Your bag is open."

Through gritted teeth, I reply, "Yes, thank you, there's nothing in it."

And then I leave behind that passenger, that Good Samaritan of the Year, bewildered by my laissez-faire response. They shrug their shoulders, turn around, insert earbuds attached to their smart phones, and return to their insular lives. Five minutes later, another rider will tap me on the shoulder to tell me the same thing, setting off an inane assembly line of activity spanning the duration of my forty-minute commute home.

I don't know why I thought leaving the zippered pocket empty would deter bystanders from tapping my shoulder, but I did. At one point, I even considered writing, "There's nothing in this pocket. Please leave me alone!" on the tape. But then I realized it wouldn't do any good if the tape was going to peel off anyway. Again, I have to ask myself the question, why waste all this time and energy conjuring up ways to hide an enormous tear that can't be concealed? Why not use another bag? Or buy one? Wouldn't that make more sense? Why don't I care about myself?

I put my body, something I already own and don't have to stand in line in the department store to purchase, in danger all the time. The irony does not escape me. But that's OCD. What you choose to worry about and what you choose to ignore never makes much sense.

↭

My childhood and teenage years offer many insights into why, forgive the schmaltzy statement, I don't love myself. When, at the age of eleven, I moved in with my father, I thought that was where I wanted to be. We shared a unique connection. He appreciated my empathic, gentle qualities, my love of classical music, ragtime, and jazz. On weekends we traveled into the city to attend a children's concert series at Lincoln Center. We'd walk next door to the performing arts library to listen to warped recordings of *Peter and the Wolf*. On the drive home, we had animated discussions about the instruments used and how this affected the mood of the piece. My father delighted in my inquisitive nature, and I reciprocated his affection by nicknaming him "Pop." Calling him Dad or Daddy just didn't do our special relationship justice.

From the moment she met me, my future stepmother sensed how captivated I was by the arts and by language. While dating my father, she worked feverishly to tap into and cultivate those interests. She let me play hooky from school to take day trips to the theatre and museums and introduced me to the whimsical literary voices of Eudora Welty, Carson

McCullers, and Isaac Bashevis Singer. But while she was busy enticing and winning me over, she was also critical of me in front of my father. She pointed out that I behaved inappropriately in social situations, didn't dress well, and was overweight. She suggested that I go to Weight Watchers. I was twelve. Nothing seemed off-putting to my father about a puffy child, who had barely reached puberty, being cheered on by a group of middle-aged men and women after stepping off the scale to announce she had lost another two pounds that week. When I was in junior high, I asked my father if he would buy me contact lenses. He replied, "Beauty has to be earned."

Like me, my father was a fat kid. He struggled with weight during his childhood and most of his adult life until he met my mother. She was also overweight. The two them went on diets and developed a passion for bike riding. Then he developed a paltry, regimented attitude towards mealtimes. For breakfast, he would consume a meager serving of half a grapefruit and a corn muffin. I'm sure there must have been, but I am hard-pressed to recall a time that he deviated from this routine.

I believe that my father had the best intentions. He didn't want me to struggle with weight into my adult life the way he had. When he likened his meal regimen to that of a dog's, telling me that if you wanted to lose weight and keep it off, that you couldn't be excited by food, I should treat it like a bowl of kibble a dog eats every day, I have to believe he did this out of love.

As I got older, the special relationship I had with him faded away. This didn't happen all at once, but I would find myself in moments alone with him when he might otherwise be supportive and encouraging, and instead he was resentful and mean-spirited. Through my teenage years, as more of these moments occurred, I became more insecure and self-loathing towards my physical appearance. I ultimately became incapable of seeing myself, the way my therapist has referred to it in the past, as a sexual being.

The summer after I returned home from spending my junior year in Israel, I had gained a significant amount of weight. There was a kiosk on the site of the Israeli school's campus that sold falafel and shawarma, a fatty, greasy cut of grilled meat that rotates on a spit until it's served. Both the falafel and shawarma were stuffed in pita with French fries (in Israel and some other countries called chips) and loaded with spicy, mild, and savory dips and mayonnaise-based sauces. I ate a lot of pita and chips while I was away. I also ate a lot of chocolate spread on white bread, chicken schnitzel, and Bamba, an Israeli snack—a peanut butter flavored puff. And Bissli, a crunchy snack food similar to Frito Lays that came in barbecue, pizza, and falafel flavors.

I had let my hair grow long, and wore flowing skirts and dress-es down to my ankles with a scuffed-up pair of brown leather sandals that I found in an Arab market in Jerusalem and made my feet bloat in excessively hot temperatures. When I arrived home from the airport, my stepmother said, "You look like you've been living in the Amazon."

I showed her my yearbook and she saw the scrawled notes from my classmates wishing me well, and the nickname my friends had given me, Jenny-Bagel, meant to suggest how fun-loving, sweet, and silly I was.

My stepmother asked, "Why do they call you Jenny-Bagel? Is it because you have such a round, fat face?"

That same summer, I was accepted to a month-long writing intensive where I studied poetry and playwriting. While attending, I was to live in the dorms and dine in the cafeteria. And so, my father made arrangements to have my food intake monitored. He compiled a customized meal plan and administered it to the staff before I arrived. The menu permitted the following foods: for breakfast, Grape Nuts and cottage cheese; for lunch, salad from the salad bar and any fresh, raw vegetables; for dinner, grilled lean meats and vegetables. Once a week, I was permitted to order steamed chicken and shrimp with brown rice from the local Chinese takeout restaurant.

I became so bored of the meals that I stood in line at the salad bar and created elaborate sculptures. I would use cheddar cheese cubes and bacon bits as brick and mortar to hold the structures together. One time, a staff member marveled over my efforts and asked me if I was a visual arts major.

As a result of my father's food regimen, I lost all the weight I had gained, and probably ten pounds more. By the time summer was over and I was preparing to return to Israel to complete my senior year, my long hair had been cut into a shorter, shoulder-length bob, and the brown leather shoes were packed away in my duffel.

When I arrived at Ben Gurion Airport in Israel on a late August afternoon, I was greeted by the staff. Ophira, our housemother, exclaimed with unabashed delight, "Jenny, where's the rest of you?"

Perhaps I should have felt proud and excited. I had endured my father's intensive weight boot camp and had achieved the desired results. But instead, I felt exhausted, battered, and confused. In my father's eyes, beauty had to be earned, but in everyone else's eyes, it was always there to begin with. I began to loathe the expectations of physical appearance, material and otherwise. I viewed myself as less while in his care, and it only worsened as I grew older.

So take this and couple it with my fear of contamination, and it's not difficult to surmise that as a teenager and now an adult I've struggled to be intimate with people. Allowing them to touch me has always been a challenge. Just as I feel unworthy owning anything nice, or looking good wearing anything new, I can't fathom how anyone could see anything other than what I see in that dressing room mirror.

My aversion to dating and entering into a relationship is why I believe I have never made a consistent effort to lose weight. I've been on many diet plans and worked with nutritionists, but never with any strong intention of feeling good about myself, and rarely by holding myself accountable and behaving in a compliant manner. I think perhaps this is because for so many years I felt controlled by expectations. As an adult, I finally have had the option to say "Fuck you!" without anticipating any type of emotional or psychological backlash.

Now obviously there are situations where I must make at least some effort to look attractive. I'm not so resistant and scarred that I completely ignore this reality. Job interviews, weddings, other special occasions, and the extremely rare instances where I go out on a first date, are times when I try, but they are not without difficulty.

To be perfectly honest, I'm sure I'm not the only person, or only woman, who feels this way. Trying to look attractive is a nuisance and annoyance. It makes me want to cry, scream, and crawl up in the fetal position. I'd rather grow the hair on my legs long enough for birds to be able to roost in it than shave down to the roots and nick myself using an apparatus that feels like a cheese grater against my bare skin. However, the social mores of Western society, especially when it comes to women, enable a certain stigma. Anyone who sees hair growing in places where nothing more than stubble should be present screech over such an abomination.

So I try, in spite of constantly fighting the open, festering wounds from my past, to adhere to these social conventions. Except during the winter, I shave my legs and armpits. I wear a blouse to an evening affair. I attempt to stuff my rolls of fat into pairs of control top stockings, which rip in the toe and the thigh as I battle the thin, delicate material to keep it from slipping back down to my feet.

Femininity, whether as a direct result of my childhood and teenage years or for other reasons unbeknownst to me, is not one of my strong points. I favor the boorish behavior of the male species over "acting like a lady." Feeling good about oneself and one's appearance should be a gender-neutral issue. For me, however, it simply isn't. I recognize there is more to the story than having an anxious temperament and opposition to the social demands that have historically instructed women to suck it up and fall in line.

Now that I'm in my forties and have recently experienced a life-threatening health scare, I'm doing more than simply trying to fight these inner demons. I'm working with a trainer to maintain my health and prevent other chronic health conditions from developing. On my fortieth birthday, before venturing out to celebrate with friends and family, I sent an email of inquiry to an organization that facilitates what is referred to as surrogate therapy. Surrogates teach individuals who struggle to be intimate how to become comfortable with their bodies, to see themselves as sexual beings, to learn how to flirt, how to experience pleasure, and to feel safe in intimate situations. Since then, I've had a Skype call with the director of the program and my therapist has also had a call to address all of her questions on the focus and goals of the program.

Though I haven't committed to taking these next steps yet, I'm still considering it. But as I continue to ponder the pros and cons, I need to make sure of one thing: that I stay away from dressing rooms for a while.

CHAPTER 6

Forty-Eight Hours

"Back so soon, Ms. Epstein?" the nurse behind the desk asked.

"Yes," I said, meeting her eyes with a glare, "I'm having surgery."

"Oh." She pursed her lips. And the paperwork was processed more expediently than the day before.

Then I sat in the waiting room. Less than five minutes later, a twenty-something male technician appeared to escort me into a small, glass-paneled room.

"What brings you to the ER today?" the technician asked nonchalantly, wrapping the blood-pressure cuff around my arm

"Surgery for obstructed kidney stones." I watched him notate the reading onto a chart and un-Velcro the band from my arm. My mom was waiting outside the triage area to join us.

"The ER attendee I saw when I was here yesterday only did an ultrasound, no X-ray or CAT scan. He thought they would pass on their own," I continued.

The technician walked us down a long corridor to the next staging area. He was short with stumpy legs but carried himself with a poised, confident gait. His boastful strides hurried us down the antiseptic-smelling hallway.

"We don't like to do those because of the radiation," he said.

I could hear my mother's almost inaudible scoff in the background as she joined us. "That's a load of crap," she said once the technician had left us. "That's the insurance companies cutting corners. A CAT scan is the gold standard of preventive care."

My mood had grown increasingly subdued throughout the day as I navigated from one crisis to the next, beginning with gagging on a Percocet and vomiting up a half gallon of water onto my favorite Pendleton blanket at 6:30 A.M. and ending with telling the driver that instead of returning to the doctor's office, he should take my my mother and me directly to the hospital, where Dr. Rinal's (pronounced "Renal") urgent voicemail had instructed us to go.

As we settled in, a flurry of activity followed. An entourage of administrators, physician assistants, and nurses entered the curtained-off staging area, some two or three at a time, to ask me dizzying strings of scripted questions, record my current prescriptions, and take a medical history. This relied on my hazy memory of having outpatient procedures to remove a pilonidal cyst eighteen years earlier, my wisdom teeth extracted shortly after that, and a benign breast biopsy in 2013 that was ordered specifically to assess my excessively fatty tissue.

No, I told them, I have never been in the hospital before.

Then I was handed a gown while a gruff Jamaican woman collected all my clothes (including my socks) and stuffed them in a bag. She said I could pick up my personal belongings from security once I was discharged.

I held onto my phone, which was bringing me great solace, as my coworkers had been briefed on the situation via text and were sending me words of encouragement. My body, riddled with the pain and trauma of the past two days, coupled with the knowledge that my friends were all thinking of me, caused me to release a few short sniffles, and I began to weep softly. This was a good distraction from the woman in the bed next to me. She sat upright, exposing the festering, flaky, scaly skin of her ballooning leg and foot.

I swallowed hard, recoiled on the cot, and gulped down the urge to gasp. My eyes wandered from my phone's screen to her leg. Gangrene? A flare-up of diabetes? The possibilities were endless.

"We need a urine sample."

Now?

"We don't know why," said the man, who I assumed to be a young resident. His manner communicated that it was just more hospital bureaucracy that he was beholden to follow.

He continued, "We need you to go while you're still in the ER. Once you're moved over to the OR for surgery, we won't be able to get the sample."

"Better do it now before they hook you up to an IV and you have to carry the pole around with you," my mom said. I sighed, defeated, and asked where I should go.

"There's a restroom over there," one of the nurses said, handing me a cup already prelabeled with my name.

Given my marching orders, I let out another deep sigh and proceeded to the ER's public restroom, my bare feet slapping across the cold linoleum floor. I stopped short at what appeared to be a trail of golden yellow trickling out from under the doorframe. The floor was soaked in urine, my socks had been smuggled away, and there was nothing to safeguard my feet from the saturated bathroom floor. At least urine is sterile, I thought, gripping my sides in agony and carefully shutting and locking the door behind me.

Under normal circumstances, contact with any bodily fluid would have left me cowering and trembling. Under normal circumstances, an innocent puddle of urine would appear to stretch the length of the Aegean Sea, and a few small streaks of excrement left behind on a toilet seat would warrant a scatological study. But these were not normal circumstances.

At 5 P. M., I was hoisted onto a gurney and wheeled over to the operating room, a plastic shower cap over my head. My mother's scowl—which earlier had concealed embarrassment over the mauled paper scraps, uncapped pens, and mateless glove removed from my backpack before the nurse took it away—had transformed to a pensive stare.

Dr. Rinal, the urologist who had diagnosed me with obstructed kidney stones, was waiting for us when we arrived. Short and stocky with glasses, Dr. Rinal had a playful smile and boisterous demeanor that made me feel at ease. Like the triage technician, he swaggered, only his swagger was amused, not contemptuous. The notable jocular temperament he had displayed earlier in the day was no longer present. His face, like my mother's, emanated concern. He apologized that the OR was backed up; it would be a while before we could get started, so I should relax. I leaned my head back against the gurney's cold slab of sterile metal plating and let Dr. Rinal's words wash over me. I was able to hear what he was saying, and at the same time, unable to hear anything at all.

"Open your mouth, please. Any metal or loose teeth?" the anesthesiologist asked. Less than a day before, I'd had the molding for a new permanent tooth put in following yet another unexpected procedure to repair a root canal. Apparently that hadn't offered enough medical traumas.

"No," I said, "just a temporary filling." My feelings of calm disassociation were being replaced with the incessant need for nervous chatter. "I have very tricky veins," I told the anesthesiologist, "very small and tricky veins."

"It will be okay," she said in a heavy Eastern European accent, Russian or Polish, "we've done this before."

She was trying to help. And she did, until I remembered that she was scheduled to puncture my noted small, tricky veins with a sleep aid from which, in rare instances, people never wake up. And so I had to wonder, was she really trying to help, or just being dismissive? Was this part of her training? Mocking my nervous chatter? Laughing at my amateur coping skills?

I wasn't just scared anymore, I was angry too. I wanted to stand on top of the gurney, let my bare ass hang out the back opening of my gown, shake my fists, and scream: *"Don't you know how terrified I am?"* But I was in too much pain to roll onto my side, much less stand on a gurney. So I did the next best thing. I lay there feeling enraged, indulging myself in an interior monologue more vengeful and deluded than a Shakespearean character's.

At this point, my small and tricky vein was punctured and the anesthesia administered. It was too late to retract my signature on the consent form. If I spent the rest of my life in a vegetative state, or didn't wake up at all, the patronizing anesthesiologist would be held harmless, completely within her right to tell the next incoming patient, frightened as they might be, that it would be okay. She had done this before.

↬

It was okay, and I did wake up.

My mother and Dr. Rinal were with me in the recovery room, talking as I lay on the gurney, woozy and disoriented.

"Could she develop pancreatitis? My husband did, after taking Cipro," my mother said.

"No," Dr. Rinal said, "that's a very rare side effect of the drug." Shifting his weight from the left foot to the right, he informed us that following the ureteroscopy and cystoscopy, I would be monitored for thirty minutes in the recovery room. If I showed any signs of infection, I would need to be taken to the intensive care unit for observation. If I didn't, which was what he expected because I was young and strong, I would be admitted to a standard hospital room. Even though I couldn't will my body to reject every microbe pathogen and other illegal squatter, I enjoyed a challenge. If I did succumb to infection, it would not be without a fight.

Relieved that I was still alive, my mom's skin tone restored itself to a normal shade of human pigment. Confident that I was in good hands, she announced she was leaving for the night.

"No, don't do that," I whined. "Wait until they take me to my room." I was confused, uncomfortable, and wanted my mommy there to do her job: mother me. I was ready to throw a tantrum to keep her from leaving the room if I had to.

"I need to head back to my apartment so I can pick up some clothes."

"Can't you wait a little longer?" I pleaded.

"Okay, fine." She threw her hands up and stormed out of the recovery room.

I sat up abruptly, but she had already disappeared into the shadows. I sighed, leaned back, and told the staff member monitoring me that I needed to call her. Then I remembered that I had given her my backpack to hold while I was in surgery. My phone was in that bag.

"I need to call her!" I said again. I was worried, but I was angry too. Where had she gone? Back to Manhattan? Or maybe just to buy cream puffs from the 7th Avenue Donut Shop? She loved those cream puffs. Jesus, who had just had their innards sliced up, her or me? Each wave of worry and anger caused my temples to throb, my hands to shake, and my chest to tighten. Was this fear, or the first symptoms of a sepsis infection?

"Here," the attendee said. "You can use this phone."

Frantically, I dialed the number. But of course, she wasn't answering.

"Mom," I said, leaving a voicemail, "don't worry about it. I wasn't thinking about how long and exhausting the day has been for you. Go. Don't worry. I'll be fine. Love you. Bye."

Because I had lived with my father during my adolescent years, I'd only begun to rebuild the foundation of a thriving mother-daughter relationship. So naturally, in complicated situations like this where both my mom and I were being tested, it was impossible for either one of us to know exactly what was the right thing to think, say, and do.

The attendee ran the thermometer over my forehead. "Looks good."

I was alert, fever-free, and ready to be taken up to my room for the night. Just as the attendants were preparing to transport me out, my mother and her repurposed complexion returned with my bag.

"I told you it was okay to go." I was exasperated. I was relieved, too, but would never give her the satisfaction of knowing that.

"And I told you I would stay," she said, forcefully handing the bag over to me.

An orderly wheeled me into the elevator, and we rode up to the floor where I would be staying for the night. It was a standard hospital room, just as Dr. Rinal had predicted. Ms. Jennifer Epstein was written on a label outside the door. The orderly lifted me off the gurney into my hospital bed.

The first thing I noticed was that my feet, thighs, and legs were swaddled in some sort of protective covering. What the hell? Was I really so out of it that I had failed to notice someone putting a pair of leg warmers over my feet? Had I been chosen to appear as an extra in a Jane Fonda workout video—the fat extra in the video that the camera occasionally pans to as a way to boost morale? *See, if I can do it, so can you!* she cheers boisterously, shooting a toothy grin into the camera. I was now sweating profusely. I thought I could feel beads of perspiration forming between my toes.

I was in what the insurance form referred to as a semiprivate room, but the sounds of labored breathing and hacking from the woman in the bed next to me—and the zombie killings from the marathon of *Walking Dead* episodes reverberating from her personal TV—felt like nothing even remotely close to semiprivate. And the only thing more oppressive than the relentless stream of unintelligible cries from zombies searching for their next victim was the stiflingly hot temperature. My bed was positioned between a heating system—a system that appeared to be controlled solely by the hospital maintenance staff—and a locked window. I focused intently on the ticking of the wall clock and fixated on when its second hand would finally reach morning and I would be able to leave this place and return home.

Eventually, the groaning of zombies transitioned to sounds of fitful cycles of loud and labored sleep-apnea-induced snoring. My roommate, whose name still hadn't been revealed to me, drifted off to sleep in fifteen to twenty minute cycles. After the second or perhaps third cycle, she peeled back the curtain partitioning our beds (which provided the illusion of privacy) in order to enter into my area and tinker with the heat.

I could hear how frustrated she was feeling through the hollow groaning sounds she was making under her breath and her laments of "how fucking hot it is in here." Satisfied with her efforts, she stumbled back to her area, violently closed the curtain, and let out a loud sigh. Her body thrashed around, furiously searching for a comfortable position. It felt like only moments later the next fifteen-minute cycle of wheezing and snoring commenced. Now that she was sleeping, I could return to the real task at hand: watching the wall clock. The hypnotic movement of the second hand was ticking towards my freedom. I shifted my head and weight around in the bed so that I could maintain my focus. *Keep following it,* I thought to myself, *you're almost there.*

Not long after, a young blond woman I recognized from the clown car of ER admissions crew came into the room. She was soft-spoken and kind. She didn't look bored or like someone who'd rather be anywhere else but there. Nope, she looked like someone who genuinely cared. I guessed she must have been serving as some sort of client coordinator or liaison.

"Why aren't you sleeping?" she asked. "Do you want me to get you an Ativan?"

"No," I said, "I don't need anything."

She remarked on hot it was in the room. "I don't know how you can stand it."

I began to make sense of why my roommate slept in cycles after I heard what sounded like a Good Humor ice cream truck ringing down the hall. Was someone bringing us a late night snack or crossword puzzles? No, it was the hospital checking my vitals every three hours. They weren't going to come back if I was sleeping, either. Instead, they would brashly pull back the curtain behind which I lay, command me to sit up, extend my arm, and open my mouth—a regimen that was impossible to shirk no matter what the circumstances.

I was obedient and alert throughout the night shift, but by around six in the morning, that bell signaled trouble. I hadn't slept in two nights and had kicked off the bedcovers because it was so oppressively warm. My leg warmers were about to disintegrate they were so saturated with perspiration.

"Mrs. Epstein," one of the night nurses said in a slow Jamaican accent, "it's time to take your vitals."

I felt weak, and my mouth was dry and rough as a steel wool pad fresh out of the package. I struggled to turn my head and prop myself up. I extended my arm, which had turned red and blotchy and was soaked with sweat from the stifling heat, and managed to let the thermometer dangle out of the side of my mouth. This required what felt like an unprecedented level of stamina.

The thermometer beeped and the technician's eyes went wide. "You have a fever. I better tell the doctor."

"No!" I said, sitting up abruptly. "It's so hot in here! The heat is on too high!" But she disappeared with the Good Humor wagon. My gaze returned to the wall clock. 6:04 A.M. Mom would soon be back to take me home.

Moments later, the supervising nurse on duty rushed in with two extra-strength Tylenol and a Dixie Cup of water. I was allowed to drink? I hadn't yet had a sip from the pitcher of water stationed next to my bed.

"Take this," she said sternly, "the doctor's worried. We have to get your fever down."

"No, it's just that it's hot in here. My temperature goes up when I'm hot." I gripped the Dixie cup in my hand and swallowed each pill anyway. My explanation was falling on deaf ears.

"I'll be back." She smiled at me and turned away.

Less than an hour later, she was looking at me pensively, once again inserting the thermometer in my mouth. It read 97.2.

"See," I boasted, "I knew I was just hot."

"Good," she said, and returned the thermometer to its holder.

I looked down at my arm. The IV had been knocked out. "Umm . . . excuse me," I said sheepishly. "I think I need a new line."

The nurse gasped. "How did that happen?"

"I don't know." This fact wasn't surprising. I wasn't exactly known for treating my body respectfully and gently. Friends or my mother would ask why I was so rough on myself. Feathers would start molting after the first week of wearing a down coat, and patterns of ink even Rorschach couldn't interpret marked shirts from which tags had just been removed.

Flustered, she told me again that she'd be back. When she returned, I repeated to her what I had said to the anesthesiologist. I did have very tricky veins, very small, tricky veins. Not only did I have small and tricky veins, but also a swollen arm displaying patterns of purple-speckled bruising from the number of times my blood had been drawn over the course of the last two days.

"Are you on blood thinners?" she asked.

"No." Then I whimpered and winced as the newest in a series of punctures was added to my arm. Why would I have thin blood? What was she trying to say? That it wasn't just my kidneys that were the problem, but some other underlying condition as well?

It was now fully morning, and daylight enveloped the sky outside my hospital room window. At 8 A.M., one of Dr. Rinal's residents, Cute Resident Robert, came to see me. He sat cutely in the armchair across from my bed. He was smiling, not a saccharine smile, but a cute smile that made me swoon and smile right back.

"How are you feeling, Jennifer?" he asked.

"Fine," I said in an upbeat voice. "I'm ready to leave."

"You gave us quite a scare."

"I was just hot," I said. "My fever came down right away."

His smile changed into a stern expression of concern. A feeling of calm disassociation took over my body again. "I'm sorry," he said, "but you're not going to be able to go home today. You need to be fever-free for twenty-four hours before we can release you."

"Aww," I said, "I feel great now. I'm not in any pain at all." I ended with a cock of my head and another smile. Maybe I could cajole him into signing off on the discharge papers.

He leaned back in the chair. "Don't spend too much time in bed today. Beds are for sick people, and you're not a sick person. Get up and walk around or sit in the chair. If you lie in the hospital bed too much, you could develop breathing problems or pneumonia."

Clearly, Cute Resident Robert had meant well. Those were words of encouragement, right? But not if you end the statement with, "If you lie in the hospital bed too long, then you really will get sick." That's exactly the opposite of what you say to someone with OCD. Dear adorable but foolish Resident Robert, not only was I now ready to jump out of the bed, but I was already plotting my escape route out of the hospital. Pneumonia! Are you kidding me, you handsome, silly man? I will tunnel my way home!

Instead, I waited. And as I waited for my mother to arrive, my anonymous roommate received several visits from medical staff, each delivering a surge of bad news, everything from there being too much protein in her urine to her procedure being pushed back to Monday. She, too, would not be getting discharged today. I started to piece together that she had been hospitalized for pneumonia, which explained all the wheezing and labored breathing. She was also experiencing complications with pregnancy, which had added time to her stay. She had a young son from whom she had been separated for the past month, and she was on leave from her job because of her illness. Regardless, the novelty of spending all day watching *The Walking Dead* and having friends sneak her Big Macs during visiting hours had worn off. She was working on getting her discharge papers pushed through and would leave against medical advice if she had to.

Listening in on these conversations left me agitated. When my mother arrived, ready to take me home, I told her they weren't letting me leave. I suspected they were trying to hold me against my will, like the imprisoned woman in the bed next to me.

My mother, who seemed rested (or perhaps properly medicated), was in a much more pleasant mood. "Believe me, Jenny," she started. Much to my chagrin, she had never stopped calling me by my childhood nickname, even when I reached adulthood and urged her not to do so. "Believe me, Jenny," she said, "hospitals are not interested in keeping you any longer than they need to. They always want to free up a bed."

Furrowing my brow, I indicated that I was skeptical of her theory, but relented and sent her away with a key to my apartment (she had been in such a hurry that morning she had left her copy at home) so she could gather a few things I might need for another night's stay: my journal that I probably wouldn't write in and the Mary Karr memoir I was reading. I might open the book and stare at the same passage for twenty minutes before moving on, meandering off onto different paths.

After my mother had gone to my apartment, I met one of the day staff nurses. She was plump and plucky with long, auburn hair. She, too, had a swagger in her step. When I told her my doctor's name, she said, "I've heard good things about him, it's the other one in his practice you need to stay away from." Taken aback by her brazen lack of professionalism, I pressed her for the reason. I gathered as much information and sordid details as I could about staff members I might encounter in the future.

This nurse would have the esteemed pleasure of emptying out my catheter. "Wow! Great! That's a lot of urine!" she exclaimed ecstatically. I practically glowed with pride.

When my mother returned, she and the nurse showed me how to walk with the IV while simultaneously holding on to the catheter.

"Hold it by the handle," the nurse said. "It's like a little purse." How unaware I was that biohazard bags were trending this year.

During the day, I followed Resident Robert's instructions and alternated between sitting in the chair and walking the halls. In one hand I held the pole connected to the IV, and in the other, my biobag. As the end of visiting hours drew near, I felt I had mastered this and was now a real pro. My bigger concern was now to ensure that my temperature remained stable each time the Good Humor wagon made its rounds.

I was excessively worried my body would fail me and cost me another day in that place. Plus, the staff had been unable to locate one of my meds in the hospital pharmacy: Viibryd, a newer and higher-class antidepressant. The other, Zoloft, was being filled off schedule and couldn't be administered until later that night. There was no danger I would go into with-drawal, even if I missed one, or even three or four doses; the medication would still be in my system. This was something I knew full well, and it would be irrational to think otherwise. But with OCD, of course I'm going to think irrationally, and so I convinced myself that without being able to swallow that little blue oval tablet, my shield of armor, there was no telling what I'd say, feel, or do. Without taking the medication, I couldn't even use the placebo effect to dupe myself. It felt, at that moment, that I had no control over my fate.

Right before dinner, after a rousing day comprised of sitting, standing, and then sitting again, I started to feel unusually fatigued. *Oh no*, I thought, *this can't happen. I can't get a fever again.* My brain began to scheme over what I could do to stop it. Drink a gallon of cold water? Suck on a bag full of ice chips? Something, anything, that would help regulate my temperature.

The bell signaled the Good Humor wagon was approaching, and the hair on my neck began to bristle. Would this be it? Was I doomed?

"Open up," said the nurse who had helped me with my biobag. The thermometer beeped 99.8. She looked at me sternly.

"99.8 is still okay, but if it goes above 100 we'll have to let the doctor know."

I grimaced, sighed, and nodded. I knew this only too well. Relieved that I had at least dodged a bullet temporarily, I gorged on my meal of chicken breast, whole grain brown rice, lentil soup, green salad, and fruit. My mom, who had been there all afternoon, looked aghast as she watched me eat.

"Slow down, Jenny," Mom said. "Relax."

But I couldn't relax. Gluttony was the only thing keeping me calm.

After dinner, my mother helped me get ready for bed before visiting hours ended. I didn't have my toiletries from home, and so she pulled out a basin resembling a bedpan from the nightstand. In it were displayed an array of complementary supplies.

"You can use these!" she said.

My nose wrinkled at the generic flavors of toothpaste, shampoos, and conditioners containing sulfates. In general, I was a snob when it came to personal care products. When my mother spread a huge glob of radioactive-green toothpaste onto my brush, I almost gagged at the sight. And the smell—a cross between spearmint and bleach. I had a full on attack when the bristles made contact with my tooth enamel. Pointing to the water pitcher, I signaled to my mother to pour so that I could spit the contents out into the bedpan bowl.

"Blech!" I exclaimed, swiping furiously at the remnants of paste foam from the corners of my mouth. "Disgusting!"

Soon, my mom left and the blaring zombies on the TV returned, making it impossible to focus on my book. But rereading the same paragraph and failing to move on to the next kept me preoccupied from obsessing over how I would pass my vitals check when the Good Humor wagon made its rounds. Again.

I rang the call bell to alert the supervising night nurse. I wanted her to help me change out of my hospital gown. My mom had told me that's what they're there for, and that I shouldn't be embarrassed to ask for help. I had been wearing the same gown since right before I went into surgery, and I wanted to spend my second night in a fresh one. It wasn't so much to ask, really, was it?

The night nurse arrived, and I told her what I needed. She said she was busy making rounds, but promised she would be back, that she wouldn't forget. I trusted her and felt reassured, but for good measure, I also added that I was feeling agitated and could she please bring me an Ativan on her way back from doing rounds. She told me she would.

I started to rub my stomach. A binding sensation was building, rumbling its way through my body, no doubt compliments of the hospital food that needed to be expelled, and soon. The catheter wasn't going to help me with this.

I slid to the edge of the bed, reaching for my biobag and cautiously slipping my fingers through the clutch. I lifted it up in my left hand while holding on the IV pole with my right, just as Biobag Nurse and my mom had showed me. I prepared to walk to the bathroom.

I positioned myself sideways on the toilet and attempted to push. But besides my sphincter tightening, all I could feel was the bandaging becoming looser. I tried to shift the weight of my body in the other direction but had a difficult time read-justing my grip on the biobag. Every time I pushed, the waste from the bag started to drip into the toilet. The only things I would have to show from my pilgrimage to the bathroom were tears in the bandaging.

It was mortifying. My face was flushed and I was starting to experience shortness of breath. Panic and desperation were definitely setting in. In addition to my obstructed kidneys, I was certain that an obstructed bowel was adding to my list of maladies. All the waste draining from my body would reverse itself and flow back due to my ineptitude at pushing. I was terrified.

Then the faint chiming of the bell grew louder as the Good Humor wagon reached the entrance to my room. My palms were sweating as I grunted and persisted, pushing harder, but nothing other than waste from the biobag came out. Both the supervising night nurse and Biobag Nurse were now in the room.

"Oh, you're busy," Biobag Nurse said pleasantly. "I'll wait."

I looked up at them, swallowed hard, choked back tears, and whimpered softly. "I can't go. How do I go?"

Slightly bewildered by the question, Biobag said, "You just go. You'll know when you need to."

The night nurse asked me if I wanted a stool softener.

"No," I whimpered again, as my lip began to quiver. "I want to be able to go."

I lowered my head and started to weep softly. The only thing I was able to push out were words. "I want to go!" The agitation flooding my body rose, replaced with desperation. "I want an Ativan!" I looked up from the toilet and did my best to position my body so as to not look like a crazy person. *Speak clearly, calmly, and advocate for yourself.* "I have OCD," I said, "and I'm feeling very agitated right now."

"Oh, you mean like with counting and hand washing?" said the supervising night nurse nonchalantly.

I looked up at her again, gritted my teeth and sobbed loudly. "No!" I cried out, *"Contamination!"*

"Oh," she said.

It was hard to say from the expression on her face whether I tapped into a deep sense of empathy or completely alarmed her. Would she bring me an Ativan or, when I finally did remove myself from the toilet and return to my bed, conclude that I was a danger to myself and strap me down?

Biobag Nurse, who was either completely oblivious or trying her best to stay out of the situation, peered in and said that she really needed to take my vitals. Maybe I could try to have a bowel movement a little later instead. Apparently, my room-mate, who also needed to use the bathroom, was growing impatient with me. Defeated, mortified, and flushed with anger and fear, I lifted myself off the toilet, reached for the biobag and IV, and returned to my bed. At least I could get rid of the Good Humor wagon and then sob alone without further interruption.

"98.3!" Biobag Nurse said.

She was so ecstatic I thought she was going to skip down the hall in a state of unbridled glee. Perhaps all that pushing had pushed the pathogens right out of me. Or maybe scared them off to a point where, if pathogens could talk, they would have said, "Come on, guys. Let's find another host to latch onto. This chick is crazy." Either way, at least one problem was solved temporarily.

Shortly after, the night nurse returned with the same level of urgency she had shown when bringing the Tylenol to get my fever down. She helped me change into a new gown and reattached the bandaging holding the catheter in place.

"I understand," she said. "I know it's hard."

Our eyes didn't meet through the whole exchange. I didn't believe she understood anything, least of all what I was feeling.

I thanked her for the Ativan and gently rolled over on my side so I could try to relax, maybe even get some sleep.

I sobbed softly for a while after that, intermittently rubbing my belly. I tried to soothe myself, ignoring the discomfort, and refrain from picking up the cell phone to call my mother. She had a rule that no family or close friends were permitted to call after dark with news or information that would upset her and cause her to worry. I had done this to her many times before she established that rule.

I was finally able to drown out the sounds of my roommate snoring like a wild boar and drift off to sleep for a few minutes. But I still had a mission to complete: to remain fever-free for a few more hours. I sipped water slowly, listening to the labored breathing of my roommate and the hypnotic ticking of the wall clock. I waited for the slow-speaking Jamaican woman to make her way down the hallway to check my vitals.

As the light started to creep through the window, I knew that the Good Humor wagon would soon be there. I grabbed the pitcher from the table, poured another cup, and continued to keep my gaze fixed on the wall clock. As I heard the bell ring, I took one last long sip and propped myself up. I was hydrated this time, and the leg warmers had been removed several hours earlier. Nothing was going to keep me there another night.

I listened as the nurse pulled back the curtain and roused my roommate from her fitful slumber. I was next. I was ready. I was going home.

"Mrs. Epstein?"

I turned my head towards her. "Yes."

"It's time to take your vit—" Before she could finish, I grabbed the thermometer from her hand to insert it in my mouth. I wasn't about to leave anything to chance. No missteps. Not this time.

The reading was normal. "Oh!" she said. "Your blood pressure's a little elevated."

"Only when you're around," I said under my breath as she scrawled numbers down on the chart.

"I'll let the doctor know," she said, returning the machines to their compartment. *Let them know,* I thought. *Let them know what?* That this nurse was determined to keep me confined to this room for the rest of my life?

It was daylight now. My mom would be up, but it was still very early. So I returned my head to the pillow, trying with all my might not to obsess over how elevated a blood pressure reading had to be to buy another night's stay in the Happiness Hotel. A few minutes later, I heard the phlebotomist make his way down the hall.

He approached my roommate. In an insincere and unnaturally upbeat voice, he said, "Hello! I'm here to draw your blood."

"No." Her tone was flat and hoarse. "You all have taken enough of my blood."

"So you're refusing?" His tone was sharper.

"Yes," she shot bad adamantly, "I'm refusing."

"Okay," he retorted in a singsong tone. "I'll inform the nurse of your refusal."

"Yes, you do that," she replied, muffled.

I started to devise a plan to get out of having my blood taken too. Maybe my roommate and I could stage a coup. Instead of like villagers chasing after the robber baron with pitchforks and flaming torches, we could pounce on the phlebotomist, wrestle him to the ground, steal all the syringes off his cart, and jab him to death. Anything to get us out of there.

Yes, I was definitely getting paranoid. I thought there must be a reason she'd been there for a whole month. *She's trying to warn me not to let them take my blood. She's trying to tell me not to do it, that it's how they keep you there.* What my mother said about hospitals wanting to discharge you as quickly as possible had to be a lie.

The phlebotomist rolled his lab cart over to my bed, but I cut him off before he could start tapping my arm to draw blood from whatever small, tricky veins I had left.

"I'm also refusing," I said.

"You, too, Ms. Epstein?" he said snidely. "I'll let the nurse know."

"Good," I muttered as he left the room. "You just do that."

A few minutes later, the supervising night nurse, the one who had witnessed my breakdown on the toilet the night before, entered the room. She spoke to my roommate first, who was also refusing to take the cough syrup she had been prescribed to stave off the lingering effects of the pneumonia. She also wouldn't use the medicated soap in the shower because she believed it was giving her yeast infections and causing her "coochie" to itch.

"We'll try and get you something else," the nurse said. "But you really should take the cough syrup."

"Ms. Epstein," she said sternly, "why are you refusing?"

"Why do you need my blood?" I said, alarmed. "I thought my white blood count was coming down." Before I had been admitted, my white blood count was only slightly elevated: 11.5. A normal reading is between 9 and 11, so there wasn't much cause for concern. But when they took my labs at Dr. Rinal's office, he told me that my white blood count was at 20, a dangerously high number. This was why he cautioned me that there was a chance I would have to be brought to intensive care if I showed any further signs of infection.

"It has been coming down, but it's still elevated, so the doctor wants us to check it again," the nurse said.

"Why couldn't you just tell me that?" My lip started to quiver again.

To any outside observer, I would appear like a petulant child, but in reality, I was panic-stricken, paranoid, and irate over the lack of transparency and information being parceled out to me. I did my best to appeal to her sense of empathy, again attempting to communicate that I had never been more scared in my life. I was surrounded by contamination, and it was absolutely imperative that I get out of there quickly.

Again she said, "I understand this must be very difficult for you."

This time her demeanor lacked sincerity, or at least in my unhinged state that's how I interpreted it. "Do you really?" I said. My demeanor communicated that I didn't think she had a fucking clue about how I felt. "Fine," I said, grumbling, "Go ahead and take it."

During this exchange, my mom texted me to say that she had just gotten out of the shower and would be there in about an hour. I hit call back and began to hyperventilate as I waited for her to pick up.

"Hi!" she said excitedly, "I was just getting ready to leave."

"Mom!" I shrieked. "You have to get me out of here! They won't let me leave. They said my white blood count's still elevated. I'm trapped here!"

"Jenny," she said calmly (my mother, a retired social worker, attempted to apply her crisis management skills), "if they think you need to stay another night, then you're going to have to listen to them. It's dangerous to discharge you when you're not well enough to go home."

Food service came to deliver breakfast and a menu to fill out for the next day's meal choices. Why would they do that if they were letting me go home? "But I've been fever-free for twenty-four hours," I cried into the phone.

"Okay," she relented, "I'll talk to the doctor, but if they have good reason to keep you another night, then you're going to have to stay there."

"*No!*" I wailed. "Please! You have to get me out of here."

At this cry, her tone turned sharp and I knew her patience was starting to fray. "Jenny, I have to go get ready. I'll be there soon, try to relax."

"Okay," I said, my voice faltering, "but please hurry."

"I will," she said, and hung up without saying goodbye or I love you.

I started to feel ashamed over my outburst. I knew she was feeling as scared and helpless as I was. It wasn't fair to her to act like this.

The phlebotomist returned to draw my blood. When he chimed, "Feel better!" I resisted the urge to lash out at him. I sat propped up, studied the menu, marked my selections, and waited.

Shortly, I heard Dr. Rinal's voice speaking to one of the nurses. "I'm looking for my patient, Jennifer Epstein." He entered my room, sipping coffee and smiling. Cute Resident Robert was with him, also smiling.

"Hi," I said.

Dr. Rinal sat down in the armchair and took another sip. He smiled again. "You feel okay?"

I nodded an emphatic yes.

"No fever?"

I shook my head. Nope. No fever.

"And do you have any pain?"

I shook my head again. "Feel fine," I said.

He tapped his finger on the arm of the chair and motioned to Robert. "Let her go . . . I want to see you in my office in three days," he said, holding up three fingers.

"When do I have the lithotripsy," I asked, "to break up the stones?"

"Dear," he said, chuckling and shaking his head at me, "we're just getting started. First we have to work on your kidneys. I'll see you in three days," and he walked out.

We're just getting started? What does that mean? What more could I possibly have to endure? No matter, all of that could be put aside for now. I reached for the cup of cottage cheese and the hard-boiled egg I had ordered the night before. Never had I delighted in eating such a bland meal. I couldn't stop smiling. I was going home.

When my mother arrived, she was the one in a frenzied state. Ready to deal with me at my worst.

"I can go, Mom," I said excitedly. "He wants to see me in three days, but I can go."

My mother was completely bewildered. "What else did he say? When is the next surgery?"

I repeated Dr. Rinal's statement: "Dear, we're just getting started."

This enraged my mother. "What does that mean? Why didn't you ask him more questions?"

"Mom," I said pointedly, "I don't know. He said, 'Dear, we're just getting started' and 'See you in three days.' That's all I know. Please find out about getting my clothes back from security."

My mother scoffed. "I can't believe you didn't ask him what that meant." She grabbed her purse and stormed out of the room to find the nurse.

I let out a huge sigh and returned to the bed to finish my food. None of this mattered. Not the next steps for my kidneys, not my mother's volatile reaction to how poorly I had advocated for my health-care needs, nothing. The only thing I cared about was going home.

Over the next few hours, I finally had proof. First, my IV was disconnected. Then the cute resident returned, slid on a pair of surgical gloves, inserted his finger in my crotch, and ripped out the catheter. I watched dumbfounded as the biobag and my human waste were discarded into the trash basket as if they were nothing more than a gum wrapper.

My mom returned to the room and said it would be a little while longer because they were waiting on Dr. Rinal to sign the discharge papers. She had been informed by one of the nurses on the day staff that I was going to have to be able to urinate on my own before I could leave. She also said that she'd spoken to my stepfather, who'd had obstructed kidney stones as well. He said that it took several hours before he was able to go on his own.

"Okay," I said, defiantly marching into the bathroom. Not only did I fill the entire toilet bowl with blood and urine, but also I successfully produced whatever mammoth turds had refused to excrete themselves from my body the night before.

"All done," I boasted with the same level of pride a toddler exhibits the first time they go poopy in the potty. "Can we leave?"

"We're still waiting on the discharge papers," my mother replied, flabbergasted. "You're done already?"

"Yep," I exclaimed, pulling on my jeans, socks, and sneakers. "Piece of cake."

The nurse returned with my discharge papers, which listed all the antibiotics and the stool softeners I would need to take. It was more than likely the antibiotics would cause constipation.

"If the blood turns valentine red, go to the ER," the nurse said.

I nodded as she read from a detailed list of all the side effects and symptoms to watch for. As I listened, that feeling of calm disassociation returned. I nodded compliantly, but didn't hear anything at all.

None of it, not the side effects, or the next surgeries, or all the bills for which I was going to be responsible, mattered. I was released from the hospital on Valentine's Day, exactly one week before my thirty-ninth birthday.

When I arrived home, I took a long, hot shower with sulfate-free products. Then I shaved my legs and armpits and fell into a deep sleep for the next four hours. If I did get sick again and had to go back to the hospital, then at least I would be properly groomed and well rested.

Does this look like a kid destined
to spend the rest of her life plagued by
anxiety and worry?

Me? Fear dirt? Never.

Current love interest, falafel!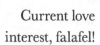

Me in Israel at the tender age of sixteen, still smiling, still not a full-fledged neurotic.

Me eating falafel

No, your eyes are not deceiving you, that is a lizard crawling up my breasts.

At an animal rescue center. The baby doe chewing on the drawstring of my jacket was a perfect ploy to keep it from licking me.

Moisture-wicking long-sleeve shirt?
Check.

REI convertible hiking pants?
Check.

Wool hiking socks, despite the sweltering temperatures?
Check.

Coconut water?
Ch—hey, wait a minute!

CHAPTER 7

H$_2$O Catch-22

"To drink or not to drink." That is the question that gnaws away at me, causing many sleepless nights. If I don't drink water, I risk ending up in the hospital again with obstructed kidney stones. If I do drink water, it could kill me.

Why do I say this? Just look at the oil leaking from the pipelines cropping up all over the country, all over the world, and en-masse contaminating our water supply. It is a truly terrifying phenomenon, and leaves me grappling with an H$_2$0 Catch-22. Either way, I risk prolonging illness or creating space for potential new diseases and neurological disorders to invade and mutate inside my body.

Like me, many of my friends follow the devastation taking place in Flint, East Chicago, and North Carolina (and the list goes on) through independent news programs like *Democracy Now!*, *The Young Turks,* and a variety of programming on Pacifica Radio stations. These friends, many of whom are activists around protecting our food and water sources, also share similar concerns. Well, perhaps not to the same level of hypersensitivity as me. I expect to wake up one morning with a third eye, but certainly, maintaining a safe water supply is of mutual concern.

Ever since my bout with kidney stones, both friends and family have been weighing in with suggestions on how to address my water intake issue. One of my friends suggested investing in a reverse osmosis water filtration system, which is one of the more effective home systems to remove the staggering number of pollutants from tap water. These include nitrates, sulfates, pesticides, arsenic, and a whole host of waterborne bacteria.

Another friend, hearing my dilemma, suggested purchasing something called LifeStraw, a water bottle designed to filter a maximum of one thousand liters, enough for one person for up to one year. In most cases, the LifeStraw is used to provide clean water to vulnerable communities in places like Kenya and India. My friend, who is a freelance documentary film-maker, used the device while traveling on production shoots to Sri Lanka and felt it might address my needs—because my affluent neighborhood in Brooklyn is certainly a clear parallel to the needs of underdeveloped nations.

When I mentioned to a friend, the one who had recommended I install a reverse osmosis system in my home, that a business in my Park Slope neighborhood carries great tasting low-mineralization water from Spain for one dollar a bottle, they thought buying water from Spain seemed excessive. But in their mind, paying a mere sum of $300 to remove unde-tectable traces of arsenic seemed perfectly sound reasoning.

Recently, I located an interactive map on Facebook that details all the neighborhoods in New York City heavily impacted by lead and a variety of other toxins. My discovery of this map happened to coincide with the first of two scheduled surgical procedures to remove more kidney stones; thankfully, a routine ultrasound caught the stones early enough that I didn't have to worry about being subjected to further hospital imprisonment. However, following the procedure, I would need to consume vast amounts of water, not an act I was eager to undertake.

Sensing that I was approaching panic mode, another friend offered to supply me with artesian well water sourced from her summer home in the Catskill Mountains. She would hand off two quart-size glass bottles of my miracle medicine, and all I would have to do was haul them back home to Brooklyn on the subway. It was a perfect solution, except that with my expected level of consumption, two quart-sized glass bottles wouldn't last more than two days, and that was a conservative estimation.

So I had no choice but to buy bottled water, which (except for the water I purchased bottled in Spain) I also didn't trust. Unless I took action in instituting the extreme measures of having a reverse osmosis system installed or was prepared to join children in Uganda sucking through a straw to remove contaminants that more than likely didn't even exist in my region of the world, I had no alternative other than to fill my conventional household water pitcher more than twenty times per day. I cringed every time this clear liquid, which aided in keeping me stone-free, entered my system.

This past winter, I purchased a PUR filter pitcher from the Park Slope Food Coop. I was apprehensive about assembling it. Much like my fear of drinking bottled water or unfiltered tap water, I was also fearful that if I assembled the pitcher incorrectly, if I didn't follow the instruction manual to the letter, the repercussions would be equally harmful. I was so apprehensive that, however long it took me to assemble the pitcher, it was the same amount of time I spent ruminating over if I should purchase it at all.

But this is not uncommon with my form of OCD, living in a constant state of uncertainty and insecurity over my decisions, fearing that my actions will hurt me instead of help. This is why I believe I have such a difficult time throwing or giving anything away: I constantly worry that if I make a mistake, even the most innocuous mistake that anyone could make, I will be punished for it, emotionally, physically, monetarily. You name it, I worry about it. So I constantly avoid putting myself in any kind of situation where I might feel the slightest bit vulnerable. And if I do put myself in that kind of situation, I appeal to the kindness of friends, strangers, and on occasion, my mother. Assembling my PUR water filter pitcher was one of those times.

It was late winter. My mother was in Brooklyn to have dinner with me, one of those rare occasions when she wasn't complaining about how stifling my apartment was, or maybe she had just shut off the valve on the radiator, I can't really remember. Because I'm single and live alone, when my mother comes to visit, I often have tasks for her to help me with, ranging from snaking the shower drain to installing light fixtures, or even alphabetizing and ordering financial documents. I depend on family and friends to guide me through these types of tasks. To them, they are simple and require nothing more than common sense, but they leave me bewildered every time. I'm not proud of being this way, but my friends laugh it off. They say, "That's just Jen being Jen. It's what makes her special, and why we love her."

That evening, I think perhaps because she was in good humor and hadn't yet felt the urge to strip down to her bra from the heat, I thought I might be able to sweet-talk my mother into tackling the project that I dreaded most of all.

I shouldn't have.

Our dialogue that winter evening began with my making the following statement: "I researched it. These filters received the highest customer ratings and are regarded as one of the top-quality filtrating systems available."

That was in response to her looking at the instructions and saying, "I don't have to go through any of these steps with my Brita." My defense received a combination sneer and eye roll.

This is where the evening entered into a steep decline. First, we learned it was necessary to soak the filter for fifteen minutes prior to inserting it into the PUR pitcher. To make matters worse, I had no drinking glasses in my cabinet in which the filter could easily be submerged. Now *I* was starting to become alarmed.

My mother pulled out a cooking pot from the bottom kitchen cabinet and suggested that we use it instead of a glass. I wrinkled my nose in protest, but, left without any other recourse, shrugged my shoulders and nodded yes. Because the pot was an oblong shape, the filter floated at the surface on its backside rather than comfortably resting and bobbing in an upright position at the top, as shown in the instructions.

"Are we doing it right?" I asked, growing increasingly concerned.

"I don't know," my mother huffed. "I never have to go through this with my Brita filter—just take it back."

I was trying to conceal the truth, that the thirty-day window to return my pitcher kit had closed and I was now stuck with this thing.

Fifteen minutes passed, signaling that the subpar soaking process had completed. We rinsed the filter off under cold water for thirty seconds and screwed the filter in. But before screwing it in, the instructions also called for washing the pitcher with warm, soapy water. This step we had both over-looked. I pointed this out to my mother, who dismissed it as unnecessary and tedious.

"You don't need to do that," she said, grunting as she continued to apply forceful pressure to the filter so that it would be secure and locked into place.

I knew it was better to shrink back from a spirited debate over this. Whichever one of us loses an argument, it is not the other one's gain. But it left me with a very uneasy feeling that if we omitted even one step, the most unthinkable disaster would descend upon both of us.

I kept seeing those words in the instructions: "Make sure to wash the pitcher with warm, soapy water before inserting the filter." The dire syntax in this sentence made me visualize bacteria breeding and growing up, over, around, and through the pitcher likes weeds in an overgrown, unkempt yard. I imagined that within days of consumption, tiny microbes would be shooting furiously out of my nose, or worse, I would soon be dead. But I've become a master of masking and internalizing these fears. While panic ensued on the inside, I worked diligently not to exhibit so much as a twinge of anxiety on the outside.

After we had affixed the sticker to the pitcher indicating when to change the filter and completed filling the cup located inside the pitcher to the recommended line, we noticed that the filter had a very slow drip. In fact, it was taking an inordinately long time to fill.

My mother puffed out her chest in disgust. "See!" she exclaimed in a high-pitched voice. "A total waste of money. It doesn't even work!"

I sighed and said nothing.

You would think after all those years of asking my mother to assist with small household projects that I would finally come to the conclusion that the exchanges never end well. In most cases, they end with the question: "What are you going to do when I'm dead?" My response is to laugh sheepishly and again avoid prolonging the conversation by any means necessary. Then my mother responds, "No, really, I mean it."

Perhaps due to the number of years we were separated from each other, my mother seems to want to impart as much wisdom as possible over an accelerated period of time. Because she might get hit by a bus tomorrow, and then who's going to show me how to store leftover vegetables in Tupperware? As a result of the onus on her, she always fails to see the humor in these situations.

After twenty minutes, the pitcher was still less than halfway filled. I opened the refrigerator door and placed it on the top rack, pushing it all the way to the back so it would be as far away from my eyeline as possible. As I shut the door to the refrigerator, my shoulders sagged in defeat.

"You're not going to use it, are you," my mother said.

"No, no," I chimed defensively, and paused. "I will, eventually."

She collected her coat and scooped up her purse from the sofa. "No, you won't." She kissed me gently on the cheek and reached for the doorknob. Then she looked at me and let out an elongated sigh, muttering, "What are you going to do when

I'm dead?" and leaving me, as she always does, with my head swimming.

Over those next months, I did use the pitcher sporadically. I alternated between the pitcher, buying water from Spain, and drinking other bottled water on which I have had the opportunity to research safety reports.

In the spring, I learned the kidney stones were back and needed to be removed through a procedure called shockwave therapy. I tell this story to my therapist with as much pathos as I can muster. I vent my apprehension of being dependent on this PUR water filter, and my fear that it may one day kill me.

I am both surprised and amused to hear her response: "Why don't you just get a Brita?"

CHAPTER 8

Restless Motherhood Syndrome

Do I want to have a child? How could I possibly? This is a question I ask myself every day. Each day the answer changes based on my age, on how well I've managed to balance my checkbook that month, or how many kids whizzing by on their scooters have run over my foot without saying they're sorry. The answer changes based on the number of friends who, after years of swearing up and down they would never have kids, call to tell me they're about to have their second, or third, or the friends who have always wanted nothing more than to have children call to tell me they have just experienced their second or third miscarriage. My answer to this question is also impacted by how many natural disasters have occurred in the last six months, signals that our planet is in peril and that we are even closer to a full-fledged crisis of global warming.

The answer constantly changes. Fears keep me up at night that my kid will have to bear the burden of my disorder, or that I will pass the symptoms of OCD directly on to him or her. In short, my answer changes as a result of any obsessive thought that envelops my head, body, and psyche in swirls of emotion and leaves me gasping for air.

These thoughts are the effects of a rare disease that I call Restless Motherhood Syndrome. There is no known treatment, though I'm sure if the pharmaceutical industry were to roll one out on the market, all the television networks would advertise without hesitation and the drug companies would make a killing. Symptoms include night sweats, biting your fingernails down to the nub until they blister and bleed, panic, delusion, recurring painful repressed memories from your own childhood, and a biological clock that never stops ticking.

I first started experiencing Restless Motherhood Syndrome when I stopped at a kiosk in the Port Authority Bus Terminal to buy a bottle of water before heading out of town for the weekend. The owner of the convenience store looked me over mysteriously and with what I perceived as a tender quality. He smiled and asked me if I was a mother. Taken aback and confused by the question, I replied no. He was astonished.

I didn't quite know how to feel. Should I have felt poised to run away in fear that he was preparing to take me in his arms and throw me down in front of the rack of pork rinds and Snyder's honey mustard pretzels and impregnate me? Should I have been offended that he was making some sort of off-the-cuff remark in reference to my rotund figure? That my zaftig shape screamed Greek goddess of fertility?

No. I didn't get that impression at all. He seemed completely genuine.

He said, "You seem like such a loving, caring person." He, the owner, was just surprised that I didn't have children.

The first symptom of RMS is the threat of biological time slipping away. Was it possible that the store owner sensed an intense longing and sadness in my voice and gait? That he somehow knew my desire to have a child had increased? Perhaps this anonymous man could feel that I was terrified by the possibility that I would burden a child with my obsessive tendencies; perhaps he had an innate understanding of how much I sincerely hope that my child will not be forced to endure the same fears I have. That is one big problem with Restless Motherhood Syndrome.

Or, if I choose to adopt or foster, which I would most likely do in order to avoid passing on any poisonous genes, another significant dilemma would be how, as a single woman on my income, I would ever manage to obtain approval from an agency. If I had a spouse to share the guilt and responsibility of fucking up a kid, then I wouldn't be so concerned.

Obviously, the intimacy issue would at some point work itself out. Then perhaps I wouldn't experience night terrors, another symptom of Restless Motherhood Syndrome, over the thought of having to discuss sex with my child. Maybe I would experience the same awkward, scared feeling every parent has when it comes to talking to their kid about sex. Who knows? It might turn out that I wouldn't even have to broach the subject of why intimacy has been so challenging for me.

If, in the end, I decide I want to take a risk and have a child on my own, what would I do if I'm still in the position I'm in now: single and nowhere remotely close to entering into a long-term relationship? My relationship quandary is because of the complications of intimacy, but also because of how much online dating sucks. I'm still waiting for my friends to set me up with someone they think would be perfect for me. I have been waiting a very long time for this to happen.

If I decide that I want to have a child on my own and am still not in a relationship, how would I get pregnant? Would I ask one of my guy friends to help me out? Do I actually have any guy friends who, in spite of how much they care about me, would ever consider getting me pregnant? I can't think of any. Would I go to a sperm bank? How the hell would I ever come up with enough money to buy sperm? I'm starting to feel light-headed thinking about it—another symptom.

Recently, however, I find myself trapped in a cycle, shifting between fear, sadness, and longing, and then moving to anger, frustration, and confusion. Then those feelings of longing change to frustration and anger when I'm late for work and unable to bypass a class of twenty preschoolers tethered together on a leash. Rather than squealing with delight in the presence of adorable towheaded children engaged in a rousing rendition of "The Wheels on the Bus," I am miffed and find myself suppressing the urge to knock them all down like a row of dominoes. Then I start to wonder, if I had a child dawdling in the morning on the way to the subway, would I fantasize about knocking him or her down too? Or even worse, leave them there in a frightened, confused stupor? (I also wonder if there's a footnote in preschool brochures that states whether they use leashes when taking students on short excursions around the neighborhood. If they do, those brochures will automatically be tossed into the rejection pile.)

When I become bogged down by these feelings, I recall a speech given by the renowned linguist and activist Noam Chomsky at an event I recently attended. I don't remember his exact statement, but what he alluded to was that the next generation will be faced with the terribly unfair burden of preserving life on a planet that is in danger of becoming uninhabitable. Even if Chomsky's morbid prophecy were proven completely false, wouldn't it be selfish to bring another child into the world to endure the effects of climate change? Isn't the world already overpopulated enough? Chomsky's prophecy makes an even more robust argument for fostering or adopting. Why should I bear a child to satisfy my own selfish needs? I could certainly nurture one who is already stuck in this world.

In the end, I have to consider to what degree Restless Motherhood Syndrome is contributing to my insatiable desire to have a child, and how much is due to societal expectations. I attribute my symptoms to the pressure I constantly feel to enter into a long-term relationship, to get married, and to have children. I often ask myself, who makes these rules? And why do I think I have to adhere to them?

This brings me back to the tale of the kiosk worker. Why was this person, who knew nothing about me or my backstory, so quick to assume that because I had a caring, pleasant aura, I was a mother? A few weeks ago, I was watching a segment on *Democracy Now!* that gets to the heart of why this kiosk worker's presumption bothered me so much.

Rebecca Solnit, a writer and activist, was speaking about her new book, *The Mother of All Questions*, which examines the many issues of living in a patriarchal world with which I have been struggling. These issues include the stigma that women face when they choose not to procreate. Loneliness is associated with being barren, whether by choice or circumstance. Solnit says, and I'm paraphrasing here, it's nobody's damn business what we choose to do with our bodies. And yet, society chooses to make it its business.

Sure, the man at the kiosk spoke presumptuously, but he also spoke tenderly and exuded genuineness. Could I have been wrong that he was simply surprised that an adult woman would be without a child? This isn't the way I look at it. From my point of view, he was surprised because he saw a nurturing, tender quality in me. I won't argue that I think I possess an innate mothering instinct, though I don't know what I could have possibly done in the kiosk so that he was able to pick up on it.

Every day, my perplexing condition brings new whirlwinds of consideration that waft over me. No money, no time, no resources, no sperm. So maybe what I'm actually feeling is anger over circumstances. And even though I teeter back and forth over the thought of bringing a kid into my life, maybe the real question is, will there ever be a right time?

I also worry about the level of success I've experienced over the years nurturing and caring for other living things. For example, pets. I worry that my child could suffer a similar fate to Murray, my betta fish. While I was preparing to leave for college, I spent many hours staring hypnotically into Murray's bowl, transfixed by his graceful, elegant movements up, around, and through the tight, murky, enclosed space he called home.

I doted excessively over him, though the cloudy condition of his tank didn't speak well of how conscientious I was at handling basic maintenance and home care. Then the day of the move came, and the car was packed to take me to freshman orientation. I rode in the back seat, holding Murray on my lap in a ziplock bag, gently shaking and sifting the contents intermittently to ensure Murray was able to maintain his movement. Everything was fine as we approached Mahwah, New Jersey, and drove through the arch welcoming us to Ramapo.

I busied myself carrying armloads of plastic crates and duffel bags up the stairs to my dorm room in Pine Hall. I introduced myself to my peers using my adult name of Jen, rather than Jenny, for the first time. As the feelings of excitement and nervousness set in, my concern for the welfare of my pet fish waned.

Murray remained in the hot car, waiting to be relieved from a growing feeling of what I assume was the certainty that I had abandoned him. When I finally did return to the car to retrieve him, I found that his once elegant movements had stalled. Well, actually, not stalled. Murray wasn't moving at all. I shook the bag a little to see if he needed to be roused. But Murray didn't move.

One of my new freshman acquaintances called out that orientation was starting. In a first-day state of confusion, excitement, and fear, I moved, unlike my beloved Murray, with impulsivity. I scooped him up, and with all the empathy and remorse of the Son of Sam, tossed him into the nearest dumpster.

I don't mention this anecdote to suggest that I would behave in such a cavalier manner towards my own child. But I'd also be lying if I said that this remote possibility hadn't entered my mind on more than one occasion. And I'd be lying if I didn't say that remote possibility scared the living shit out of me.

Because Murray's untimely death wasn't the last time that I cared for another living thing with tragic results. On my 22nd birthday, I received a pair of goldfish as a birthday present. Cheeks and Floyd were not long for this world. Only three and a half months after I received them, they, too, passed due to overfeeding. I would feed them before I left for class and then forget I had fed them only two hours earlier and feed them again. I also fed them more than the recommended amount in each serving. I shouldn't have been surprised when I returned to my campus apartment and found them floating at the surface of the bowl.

Nineteen and twenty-two are not the best years of a person's life to highlight as examples of emotional development, but at the age of thirty-five, well past the norm of child rearing, I fed our family dog Lucky a handful of cured deli pastrami and thus gave her bloody diarrhea for three days. I knew the pastrami was too rich for her to digest, and yet I did it anyway.

I have to ask myself if I would overfeed my child. Or forget to feed them. What if I received a call from Child Protective Services to inform me that they were found rummaging in a dumpster because they were hungry? What if I decided to take up foraging, and without doing any background research, fed my child an unidentified species of mushroom? What if this irresponsible, callous behavior sent them into convulsions?

Though their actions are usually loving and almost always well-intentioned, mothers, parents, make mistakes. I practically choked to death after swallowing a penny as an infant. I'm sure I wasn't out of my family's eyesight for less than a minute before crawling over to that fascinating, shiny object and sticking it in my mouth.

When I was in first grade, I performed in a school recital and my mother, well-intentioned and loving, packed a bag of jellybeans in my lunch as a good luck treat. Unfortunately, I was getting over a minor case of the stomach flu and hurled all over my sweater during a spirited solo of "You're a Grand Old Flag."

Over the years, I've made loving and well-intentioned mistakes with pets, my niece, and my friends' kids. Recently, I traveled to spend the holidays with a very close friend from high school and meet my one-year-old honorary godson. The nanny had the day off and my friend asked if I could watch her son while she took a quick shower.

Of course I would, I said. This was my chance for us to bond. I would sit in his playpen, hold him in my lap, and read him the pop-up safari books I had bought as a birthday gift. I envisioned it would be great. I would make all the funny intonations and roaring sounds as I read. He would laugh and look at me with wonder, in awe of my impeccable timing when a felt-covered puppet giraffe popped out at him as I prepared to turn the page. I would crumble as this sweet little boy put his head on my shoulder or waddled over to his favorite toy so he could hand it to me, gesturing that he wanted to share. *I can do this*, I thought, *the guy at the kiosk was right. I* am *meant to be a mother.*

Everything happened as I envisioned it would. For less than two minutes. Then my friend's son got bored and brazenly tried to crawl out of the playpen and back into the kitchen, where a pile of pots and pans that hadn't been put away yet offered more entertainment than a story about a monkey swinging across a jungle and eating bananas ever could.

I gasped, slammed and locked the gate to the play space, and scooped him up in my arms. He kicked, flailed his arms, and cried crocodile tears while I attempted to plop him back down inside again. By the time I had sequestered him back in his play space, he wasn't crying crocodile tears anymore. He was wailing, tears were streaming down his face, and he was coughing from not being able to get enough air.

"What happened?" My friend came running out, shirtless with her hair in a towel. "What's wrong with him?" she said, bending down. Her boobs jiggled over the rail as she strained to pick her son up and console him.

"He was trying to get out."

"So? He's allowed out," she said, wiping tears from his face. "He just wants to explore." She smiled and kissed him gently on the cheek.

I didn't know. How could I have been expected to know that? She didn't tell me, and I had lovingly made a well-intentioned mistake.

The next time I watched him, he was in his high chair eating breakfast and my friend was brushing her teeth. She returned to find his nose swollen and red. There was blood coming out from his tiny nostrils. I had turned my head away for a second to sip my tea and he had managed to stick his finger and a slice of apple up his nose.

"Jen," my friend said, cleaning her son off with a wet wipe. "I love you, but if you want one of these, they're a lot of work. You can't take your eyes off them, even for a second."

She was right. Having a kid would be a lot of work. Especially with my fear of contamination. If I had returned from brushing my teeth to find that my kid had stuck fruit up their nose and it was crusted with blood, the scene would have been much more dramatic. That friend probably wouldn't have been allowed to see my kid again until their Bar/Bat Mitzvah. If, at the age of thirteen, my kid was still sticking fruit in small orifices of their body, we would have much bigger problems to contend with than a bloody nose.

To answer the question: no, there is no right time or circumstance to have a child. So I'm taking steps, albeit, no pun intended, baby steps, towards making that happen.

One of my friends has a colleague who is single and recently adopted a child. I asked my friend to put me in touch with her colleague so I can learn more about the process to adopt. I also have a friend who works in foster care, so I can give her a call and request that she email me some literature on fostering. I could also rob a bank so that I can pay a sperm donor. No, never mind, scratch that. If all else fails, I can always get a new pet fish.

CHAPTER 9

Paperwork

It's impossible for me to count the number of opportunities I've missed over the years because of my aversion to paperwork. Ordering paperwork, reviewing paperwork, filling out paperwork, mailing out or faxing completed paperwork—just thinking and writing about paperwork causes me to break out in hives.

So wouldn't it make sense to just get it over with and avoid developing blistering welts all over my body? Of course it would, but with OCD, the illogical and irrational will almost always reign supreme. Whatever actions alleviate the most stress and offer the best outcome, naturally, the OCD brain will swing towards doing the exact opposite.

In the spring of 2008, I received my admissions letter to attend the Media Studies graduate program at the New School in Manhattan. I had been offered a department scholarship of one thousand dollars a semester, and the company I worked for generously provided tuition reimbursement with a fifteen thousand dollar lifetime cap and a five thousand dollar maximum per year. All I had to do was file a dozen simple forms, send out a few quick emails to my company's benefits department, and *poof*! I'd be able to usher my financial woes to the side. What ordinary everyday fool wouldn't jump at the chance to grab the brass ring and do that?

Answer: one with OCD. I didn't contact the benefits department the day I was accepted, the next, or even the day after that. I wasn't in contact after completing my course selection for the first semester, or after taking the day off from work to go down to the New School and waive the school's health insurance policy (this, by the way, required filling out several forms of paperwork). I didn't even contact the benefits department after visiting the university bursar's office to pay the first semester's tuition bill. If I had been a reasonable, responsible person, upon writing that first check, after realizing the magnitude of financial sacrifice I'd be making and burden I'd be undertaking, then, surely, I wouldn't have turned away free money. It would have put the onus on me to spring into action and make one simple call. Right? Wrong! Even the unsettling reality of massive costs did not prompt me.

It took me one year. Because I delayed, and then had to wait for all the paperwork to be processed, I ended up receiving only $11,000 before I graduated. That money was enough to cover one full semester's tuition and partially refund a second, and I could argue that I still ended up earning a healthy sum of money back, better than no sum at all, but regardless, I left $4,000 on the table that could have been used towards paying back the next ten year's worth of $40,000 in student loan debt I had acquired.

Incidentally, I had enlisted a friend who is more financially savvy then I am to research lenders and enroll me in various student loan programs. I probably could have enlisted the guy behind the deli counter who applies a smear of cream cheese to my pumpernickel bagel every morning—anyone would have been able to research those lenders and file paperwork with more ease and know-how than me.

The reason certainly has little to do with possessing the intellectual capacity to make wise, informed decisions. I'm beyond competent in this area. Rather, it is the paralyzing anxiety that I will make a mistake and that said mistake will cause irreparable harm to me, someone else, or both. The irony with OCD is that by not sitting down and employing some thought-stopping techniques (I say to myself, "You're being ridiculous. Do yourself a favor, shut up, and grab a pen"), I do end up causing myself harm.

A little over a year after returning from Costa Rica, my symptoms of OCD had improved but were still bothersome enough that my daily routine was impacted. I was tired of being late to work every day because the refrigerator, kitchen cabinets, and a stove that wasn't even in service had to be checked, rechecked, and then checked again to ensure that every knob and handle had been securely shut and turned off. That ritual took ten minutes to complete. Then, once I had actually exited my apartment, I had to check that the front door was locked. This ritual added an extra ten minutes.

But hearing the door shut and turning the key didn't satisfy all the necessary requirements to give me peace of mind; it was also necessary to grip the handle for several seconds and repeat the following words to myself, silently, three times: "I locked the door. I locked the door. I locked the door." Once that ritual was over, I could walk to the door between the entrance and the foyer and repeat the same sentence again, only this time loudly and emphatically: "I locked the door!"

I was always mortified if a passing tenant interrupted this ritual. I learned to compensate for my humiliation by saying something like, "I can't believe I locked the door and left my keys in the apartment on the kitchen counter! Now I have to get the super to let me back in. I feel so stupid!" Then I would shake my head from side to side, lamenting my foolish act.

So my therapist and I both agreed that it was time to take a more experimental approach to treat my OCD. I enrolled in a ten-week online cognitive behavioral program and was only permitted to consult with the assigned therapist during the course. The intensive program required a lot of reading, journaling, and most importantly, goal setting, one of which was to take steps to move past my fear of getting rid of documents.

Every day, I was tasked with discarding two documents, noting how it made me feel. Did it make me apprehensive? Did it cause any physical reactions? Shortness of breath, headaches, nausea? I could select any piece of paperwork I wanted; it didn't matter as long as I actually threw it out. After discarding unopened credit card applications for some weeks, it did become easier. Then I was ready to move forward with a more significant step: shredding.

The reason shredding is so much more challenging is because with the act comes an onslaught of questions I feel compelled to answer. What if I need it later? What if someone fishes one of the shredded papers out of the trash—in spite of the egg shells and fish scales—and pieces the slimy contents back together and steals my identity? Shredding requires thought and planning, responsibility, and the willingness to let something of greater or lesser value go. And because it is so difficult, I have an even bigger conundrum to overcome: clutter. This problem has repelled by mother from visiting my Brooklyn apartment for what seems like months at a time.

After I got out of the hospital, my mother stayed at my apartment for two nights to take care of me. I woke up that first morning to hear her arranging a stack of menus and a plethora of rubber bands, pushpins, pens, picture hangers, nails, and screws in the utility drawer. By the time of her second stay after my next surgery, an outpatient procedure for lithotripsy, she had organized all of the medical bills, prescription guides, discharge instructions, and lab results into three separate piles. One for the ER, another for the first surgery and nights spent in the hospital, and a third for the second surgery. Her efforts withstood my compulsion to create clutter for six months before they returned to their usual state of disarray.

But my aversion to paperwork is not completely a lost cause. I no longer run screaming in the other direction when my mother politely suggests that I call my financial advisor, Melvin, to set up a "Pay On Death" transaction. This would ensure that if I died in a plane crash tomorrow, my savings would be paid out to whomever I made provisions for. Acid bubbles don't form in my mouth when my mom makes statements like, "It's just that easy, call Melvin and he'll send you the paperwork." Come to think of it, I'm not sure she knows that I waited a year to make a call to register for tuition reimbursement. Surprise, Mom!

I recently had one major accomplishment that has helped me to move past my fear: I rolled over a 401(k) plan from a previous employer into an IRA. This, in my mind, grants eligibility to submit an application for inclusion in the paperwork hall of fame. The level of involvement, faxing of paperwork, and calls needed to ensure that the paperwork was received into the

hands of the appropriate parties hits it big time. More importantly, I removed a piece of paperwork from the towering pile
teetering on my kitchen table. In all likelihood, rolling over
the 401(k) saved me from that mammoth pile toppling over,
trapping me, and crushing my spine. Leading to what? You
guessed it, more paperwork.

CHAPTER 10

The Laundromat

"You should write about laundry, you certainly have enough material," Mom said.

My mother was right. I have no shortage of material on the subject. OCD and laundry don't mix well.

It's not that I'm a compulsive washer. Quite the opposite, in fact; I would argue I don't launder my bedding often enough. But it's the surge of decision-making and lack of control that becomes problematic. Selecting the temperature cycle on the washing machine leaves me equally anxiety ridden as shredding documents. However, my fear of contamination casts the deciding vote, and it is almost always to launder my clothing and bedding, even those made of the most delicate fabrics, on the highest temperature.

Washing your clothes on hot in a commercial washer will kill just about anything, including the material used to assemble jeans and sweaters by workers in Honduras for fifty cents an hour. The hot cycle should be reserved for extreme situations. Washing the clothing and bedding of family ravaged by the stomach flu or an outbreak of head lice are two reasonable scenarios that spring to mind, not cleaning a silk blouse.

Though the decision leaves me deeply ambivalent, and my favorite pair of Levi's subject to another hole in the crotch (always the crotch, never something trendy and cool like the knee or the leg), I will almost always pick the "special cycle." Better to leave my shirt looking like a piece of Swiss cheese than grant freedom of life to a bedbug.

The conundrum of getting to the laundromat is something most apartment dwellers can relate to. The average urbanite easily commiserates over the hassle of hauling armloads of blue canvas IKEA bags stuffed with the prior week's linens, work clothes, and unmentionables down and up the stairs of a five-floor walk-up, spilling trails of powdered detergent and dropping pairs of skid-marked Fruit of the Loom men's briefs along the way.

In my case, I substitute blue canvas IKEA bags and five-floor walk-ups for my purple drawstring laundry bag piled into the bubbe cart and dragged down the steep set of concrete steps leading out my building.

Maneuvering the bubbe cart down the steps, particularly when they are slick with ice from yesterday's storm, is certainly more cumbersome then getting it back up again, but both require strategic planning and thinking. The cart must be lifted; I cannot simply walk it or let it roll down the stairs by itself. Also, when I lift the cart, I must face away from it. Over the years I've come to rely on my peripheral vision to guide me down the stairs—and blind hope that if I slip, my ass landing inside the bubbe cart will break my fall.

I can't recount the number of times a spoke, nut, or bolt from one of the wheels has gotten caught on the cuff of my jeans and I was sure that both the cart and I would tumble down the stairs, bashing my skull and all its innards against the railing along the way. So far, though, no casualties. Only minor scrapes and bruises.

If another tenant happens to be sitting out on the steps while I'm going through this process, I will never stop to ask for help. For whatever inane reason, I consider it a badge of honor to "go it alone," to refuse depending on the kindness of strangers. Instead of clearing my throat or brushing the wheel of the bubbe cart against their shoulder to signal for help, I'll grunt and clumsily walk the bubbe cart down the steps myself. The tenant will watch nervously as this troubling scene unfolds.

"Need a hand with that?" they will ask when they see me pause to catch my breath and plot out my next move.

"No, that's okay, I've got it," I'll wheeze back in reply. "I do this all the time."

The tenant will shrug their shoulders, sigh, take another drag off their cigarette, and hope that my decision to decline their assistance will not end up with a metal grocery cart, a week's worth of laundry, and me landing in their lap.

Once I've reached the bottom step, sans fractured skull, I weave masterfully through a brigade of parked strollers outside the Bareburger on 1st Street. All that is left to do then is avoid being enticed to buy a mushroom empanada and handwoven African basket from the PS 321 flea market and wait for the light to change at the crosswalk. There lies my final destination. Then all that is left to do is survey the laundromat, stake out the highest-efficiency washer, and begin unloading.

Most urbanites have caught on by now that the words "all that is left to do" are an oxymoron. For starters, there is no such thing as a high-efficiency washer. What I do is survey the laundromat for a "working" washer.

I have watched more than my share of fellow laundromat-goers absentmindedly dump the contents of their IKEA bags into the washer and deposit enough detergent into the soap compartment to cover two loads before arriving at the bitter realization that the coin slot on the machine is broken. They'll start off confident that the situation can be remedied. Perhaps they've inadvertently inserted two dollars worth of Canadian quarters instead of standard US ones. Unlikely, yet still plausible. After examining the quarters for proof of United States mint certification, they'll insert the coins again, only to have the coin slot spit them out.

The laundromat-goer is puzzled, and understandably, growing increasingly agitated, but still not quite ready to accept defeat. Perhaps they've inserted the coins into the machine too quickly? These machines, after all, have endured their share of wear and tear over the years. Maybe a gentle touch is all that is needed.

The laundromat-goer pauses to regain their composure before offering the machine a loving gesture. They acknowledge its battle scars and, as one would with any good soldier returning home from war, thank the machine for its service.

The machine shudders and emits an unpleasant smell.

This poor dejected soul has now morphed from overconfident individual into an irate, nonsensical speaker. Kicking, banging on, and barking a slew of unintelligible obscenities at the commercial front-load washer, they must now accept they have been outwitted by an inanimate object and wait for another machine to become available.

These are scenarios where the average laundromat-goer and I are simpatico. After that, our difficulties getting our clothes and linens cleaned part ways, and my difficulties enter a world unto themselves.

I have a system at the laundromat that, except for the typical derailment of waiting for a machine to open up, must not be altered. This system includes safeguarding my clean clothing from the basket provided by the laundromat. I use a drawstring trash bag, which my psychiatrist refers to as a barrier. I have watched what other customers place in their baskets—anything from a purse to their child and their child's feet to unclean clothes, sheets, and towels. Knowing this, subjecting my clean clothing to the dirt, grime, and possibly feces tracked in on a child's shoe is not a risk I'm willing to take.

Once I have removed my wash from the machine and ensured that not one pair of Hanes briefs, knee socks, or a button-down shirt has touched the base of the basket and its contents are satisfactorily swaddled between the barrier of the trash bag, I can roll the cart over to the dryer with some semblance of peace of mind.

I should mention that dryers are not always readily available for the taking. When situations such as this present themselves, a new OCD dilemma rears its ugly head: the potential of exposing my wet, freshly cleaned laundry to airborne contaminants. Sometimes I have to wait fifteen or twenty minutes for a dryer, at which point the irrational neurons in my brain violently clash with the rational ones. "What if" scenarios seize control. What if someone at the laundromat begins to hack and cough?

What if particles of spittle from their mouth become airborne and touch down on my clothing? What if a fly lands on, dies, or lays eggs in the crotch lining of my underwear? What if it's more than twenty minutes before a dryer becomes available and my clothes begin to dry on their own? There would be no heat to destroy the eggs that would soon hatch live maggots. How would I gauge if my clothes were even clean anymore? Then I'd have to rewash my laundry and go through the whole process all over again.

Needless to say, I watch the timers on the dryers count down with the intensity and determination of a drag racer. I grip my hands around the basket, like a driver would around the steering wheel, and inch closer and closer to the machine as the minutes on the dial decrease. I position myself against the basket and roll the wheels back and forth, the way a car would accelerate on the gas at the starting line, waiting for the flag.

When the dial on the timer reaches zero, forget any disdain or ill will I might harbor towards people who remove other's laundry from dryers. This is *my* laundry. The stakes are much higher, and my clothes have begun to dry on their own. All bets are off.

"Is this one yours?" I'll motion to the laundromat-goer absentmindedly scrolling through their phone. Nope, they confirm, with a shake of the head.

I begin picking at my face, rubbing my chin nervously. I move towards the dryer, then quickly step back, retract, then forward again. If I crane my head abruptly, I can hear my neck crack as I scan the laundromat for this self-involved cretin. Maybe they're outside? I run over to the door, stand on tiptoes, and look down the block to see if they could be on their way back from picking up a coffee at Connecticut Muffin. Shit. No sign. Beads of sweat begin to form on my lower lip. I bite down to keep from screaming. Fuck it. I've been polite enough. The grace period is over. As I'm using my cart to push the other ones out of the way, that heartless excuse for a human being saunters in with a bottle of fabric softener and package of dryer sheets, completely oblivious to the state of affairs they've created.

Seething, I ask through gritted teeth, "Is this stuff yours?" and stare at the floor to deter my first inclination, which is to shove them out of way and throw their clothes into the basket. They remove each individual pair of boxers, placing each article of clothing gently into the blue IKEA canvas bag without even a sliver of urgency.

The dryer is free, but my clothes are half dry. I run my hand over my favorite shirt, feeling around the stitching and seams for any remaining areas of moisture. There's another hurdle I now need to deal with: the lint screen. The ominous lint screen has always been a painful burden for me. When I lived near Grand Army Plaza, I used a laundromat that had the self-clean lint screens. I would pull the screen out of its compartment in the dryer, shake the layers of dust, lint, pieces of stray thread, and remnants of torn, soggy dollar bills into the trash bin. This was a fail-safe plan. Any unseemly leftovers from the previous customer could be disposed of effortlessly.

Of course, only management was supposed to clean those lint compartments, but I always smiled, made feeble attempts to coerce her into letting me self-clean by offering to walk over to Met Foodmarket, the Prospect Heights neighborhood grocery store, to pick up a can of grape-flavored Fanta or whatever glucose-laden sundry might win them over.

Usually the manager would just furrow her brow and wave me over to one of the machines she wasn't using to fulfill a client order. Not only did she manage the self-service clients, but drop-offs for customers who sent their laundry out as well. Her chronic limp and sciatic nerve had no time or energy to do battle with my neuroses.

One of the things I missed most when I moved to a neighborhood further south in Park Slope was having access to self-cleaning lint screens. I considered migrating north with the bubbe cart once a week so I could continue using the machines, but in the end I decided the trip was simply too much for one layperson to endure. For a while, I implemented strategies to stave off my fears of what might be lurking. Rather than doing my laundry on the weekend, at a time when there was high traffic, I would go on a Monday morning, at 6 A.M. right after management arrived. By the time my laundry was ready to go in the dryer, they had already completed the regimen of slipping on a pair of rubber gloves, reaching into the lint screen, and extracting the prior day's accumulation of dust, lint, loose change, and lollipop wrappers. Ultimately, though, my schedule at work changed, and squeezing an extra hour into my morning to wash a week's worth of clothing simply to indulge my irrational thoughts was no longer an option. In lieu of a 6 A.M. arrival, a very specific routine must be adhered to in order to satisfy my set of fastidious and illogical requirements

First, all clothes and other laundry must remain in the dryer for a period of no less than twenty minutes. I read somewhere, though I cannot recall the source, that this is the length of time clothing, sheets, towels, and even bathroom rugs need to dry on high heat to kill bedbugs. Never once, not even in a severe time crunch, have I strayed from this rule. Then, after twenty minutes have lapsed, I burn my fingers on the hot metal zipper as I remove my pants and wave away the smoke wafting from the vents of a commercial dyer that has just completed its cycle.

I have one final task to master before returning home. Getting everything into the purple nylon drawstring laundry bag might sound simple, but one needs to consider that first I need to make sure every freshly clean and dried article either is inserted directly into the laundry bag or the kitchen trash bag I've spread out again in the basket. If a sock or pair of underwear tumbles out of the dryer and onto the floor after I've opened the door, I have to deposit a quarter into the machine and dry the tainted items another seven minutes to remove any dirt or airborne contaminants they may have come in contact with after hitting the ground.

Extreme? Yes, absolutely. I should note, though, that when I am pressed for time, I may introduce an alternative method, such as separating the underwear and socks from my other laundry and stuffing them into the bottom of the bubbe cart, wheeling everything home, and placing them on top the radiator to receive the extra five minutes of heat needed. But it's not the same. Instead of putting the underwear away with the rest of my clean laundry, I'll fold it and tuck it away in a plastic bag in the hallway closet. I won't lie on clean sheets or the sofa and only wear the underpants outside the apartment the next day so I can justify having to launder them again.

I've tried before to ignore this rule, to fold everything together under layers of clothes or on top of sports bras. Sometimes I'll use a plastic or kitchen trash bag as a liner, placing the underwear on top of the bag as a barrier, shielding my exposed pair of briefs from the bottom drawer of the wire stackable unit I keep in the bedroom. But I'll thrash around and toss and turn all night until the next morning, when I can finally shower, throw those underpants on, and thrust them away from the other ones, which hopefully remain unscathed.

Once I'm home, the final step is to fold all the washed and dried laundry that has successfully passed inspection. I never fold on the table at the laundromat everyone else uses. That would defeat the purpose.

Folding is perhaps the most relaxing part of the laundry process. It's almost cathartic to be home and feel the heat emanating off the material of a cotton T-shirt. There's no pressure to get out of one person's way or wait on someone else to free up a machine. I can take my time, breathe in the pungent scent from the dryer sheets still permeating my clothing, and savor the moment.

CHAPTER 11

Failing Upwards

I never could envision myself working with a personal trainer. Even the words "personal" and "trainer" in the same sentence exudes a certain bourgeoisie aristocratic air that someone like me who often walks out of the apartment with my shirt on backwards has no business with. People who have personal trainers have personal chefs, personal assistants, live-in sprawling estates with expertly manicured lawns, and stables filled with prize-winning Arabian thoroughbreds named Thunder Clap.

Perhaps this is an exaggeration, but at the very least, people who have personal trainers own more than three pairs of shoes. They live comfortably. They are not people like me. I live in a city overrun with people not like me. People who own businesses that excel in selling services to people not like me. Gyms, even the no-frill ones with zero initiation fees, will try to sell you a personal trainer package after you join. I always take advantage of the free session from the bronze-skinned, beefy male trainer arbitrarily assigned to assess my body mass index and determine how many years to shave off my life expectancy based on the results. At the end of the complimentary workout, a computer algorithm calculates the number of sessions I'll need to improve my balance and core stability enough to keep me from keeling over dead next week.

"Two sessions a week for thirty weeks at fifty dollars a session, that's the best deal I can offer you," he'll say. "If you don't take it and choose to work out on your own," he pauses, "it will be a lot harder when you finally *do* decide to take it."

Then I leave the gym feeling dejected, hopeless, and harboring an eerie sensation that the next steps I take outside will be my last ones. If his intention was to motivate me, he has failed.

↝

I returned home from shock wave therapy, my third surgical procedure to remove my kidney stones, still unwarmed to the idea of subjecting myself to exercise. But I did recognize that I needed help if I was ever going to reverse the downward spiral my health had taken. And so I emailed Randi, a nutritionist and personal trainer. I didn't know her well, but many of our friends were part of the same circle and a few of our mutual friends were clients of hers.

When I contacted Randi, my reason was simply to ask her if she knew of any naturopaths who accepted insurance. I really did not want to use conventional medications to tackle my issues with high blood pressure, especially since it had not even *been* an issue until I developed kidney stones. I had no way of proving any kind of correlation between the stones and my blood pressure, but I felt adamant I could improve my numbers more naturally with the right support system.

Randi wrote back that she hoped I would be okay, that she and all of our mutual friends were wishing me a good, speedy recovery, that she would love to help in any way, and (this is where I lost it and began to cry) to let her know if she could come over and bring me anything.

Between pauses to sob, I replied to Randi that I just wanted to be healthy again. She immediately went to work contacting colleagues for recommendations.

A few days later, Randi contacted me to provide an update on her search, adding how great it was that I was seeking out a more holistic alternative to medication and that if I was interested, she would love to work with me. Even though people like me don't work with trainers, there was something very different about Randi. I was intrigued, and though I was certain I would never be able to afford it, decided to go.

I arrived for the first time at the door to Randi's studio, a fifth-floor walk-up located on the Lower East Side of Manhattan, gasping for air and sweating uncontrollably. Was this part of the workout? I was ready to curl up in a corner and take a nap.

Randi had a tall glass of water waiting on the kitchen table for me, and I sipped it slowly as I scanned the room; two pairs of weights (one for wrists, another for ankles), a hula hoop, yoga mats, dumbbells, a core-strength ball, and a variety of resistance bands were lined neatly against the living-room wall next to a bookcase that displayed a copy of Howard Zinn's *A People's History of the United States* and a multitude of titles on natural healing and wellness. Next to them was a stack of board games. The air conditioner unit in the living room window, set at a comfortable sixty-eight degrees, hummed softly in the background.

Minimized on the screen of a desktop computer were a music track labeled "Jen's Mix" and a set of notes for today's workout. Hanging above the desk was a framed diploma certifying completion of a program to administer drugless therapy. On the back walls next to the French doors leading to the bedroom were pieces of duct tape forming the shape of an "X." On the floor, next to a forty-inch flat-screen TV, sat a toy plastic animatronic dinosaur.

Randi began by teaching me muscle warm-ups and breathing techniques. Within moments of the first exercise, she exclaimed with delight that I "had great breath!" Not the scent, I assumed. "I wish everyone breathed like that," she said.

Oh good, I thought. If I could receive positive feedback simply for performing a natural human function like breathing, perhaps I could stay motivated and come back for the next session.

As it turns out, breathing is complicated. Specifically, exhaling is complicated. Contrary to the way I had been taught, the proper breathing technique when blowing out air from the mouth is to contract rather than expand the diaphragm. Apparently I had been exhaling wrong for the past forty years of my life.

What started out slowly as cardio exercises running back and forth across the room unexpectedly ramped up when Randi asked me to do what is called a "pop-up." Steps involved in this exercise are as follows. Step 1: run to the wall closest to the desk in the living room. Step 2: jump in the air. And Step 3: raise your arms, reach up to touch the ceiling, and yell "Pop!" Then run to the wall closest to the kitchen and repeat steps 2-4 again. Easy.

"Awesome job, Jen!" Randi cheered. "Only fifteen more to go!"

"Ha, ha," I chuckled nervously.

"You can do it," Randi replied, nodding.

I pounded across the floor, jumping, raising my arms, touching the ceiling, and yelling "Pop!" Five more times. Six more times. I reached to pull up my shorts, which with each jump and exclamation of "Pop!" had slipped further down till they were hanging around my ankles. It was just me, Randi, and my Hanes briefs. Ten times. Twelve times.

"Pop!" I wheezed, gripping my sides, choking back bile. Fourteen times. Fifteen times.

"Great work, Jen!" Randi applauded. "Go grab some water."

We ended our workout with mindfulness, meditation, and stretching. Then we hugged sweatily and Randi showed me how to adjust the temperature in the shower. She instructed me to run the water on hot for the first few minutes to relax the muscles, then turn it back to warm.

The bathroom shelves were stocked with Q-tips, tampons, panty liners, moisturizers, a hair dryer, and freshly laundered white cotton towels neatly folded on the bottom two shelves. There was also a dream catcher hanging over the toilet and Reiki energy candles placed along the windowsill. Randi had all my favorite sulfate-free shampoos conditioners and a body-wash with a calming lemon scent stored and ready for use in the shower. Even though I was in another person's bathroom, with someone else's household dirt and strands of hair on the tile that had been overlooked during the last cleaning, I felt completely at ease. This was good dirt, safe dirt. In spite of the toilet running and the persistent drip of the sink faucet, I was able to envision myself showering there again next week.

Celtic meditation music played softly for the duration of my shower and greeted me after I finished dressing and opened the bathroom door. A heavy cloud of mist and steam followed closely behind me. While I was in the shower, Randi had put together a blend of essential oils in a small mason jar for me to take home and apply if my muscles were sore. Replacing the tall glass of water I had drunk from when I first arrived was a liquid substance chocked with dark, leafy greens. Randi had prepared a kale shake because, as she said, it was important for me to get in the habit of chewing and savoring my meals. I couldn't wait to come back.

❧

I've been working with Randi for a little less than a year now. It has not been easy to keep up the momentum necessary to work out twice a week for seventy-five minutes. That type of feat I consider a major success, that I am doing something to feel good about myself, to improve on my physical appearance, to see myself as someone worth keeping alive a few extra years. And the real success isn't exerting the required endurance to make it through the workout, it's showing up at all. It's what I refer to as failing upwards: coming right up to failing and then finding the will to make incremental changes. These are small successes, but they build over time.

Randi is just about to complete her certification as a physical therapist. She told me that our working together and my determination to write this book was one of the reasons she decided to go back to school. I now know that personal trainers work with people *exactly* like me.

I've always been a firm believer that everything happens for a reason. Even though at the time we may not understand why, we will always grow and evolve into better human beings as a result of hardship. [Note: While I was making the final revisions to this manuscript, Randi got another job… Sadly, we're no longer working together but I'm happy for her and extremely grateful that she gave me a transformative, life-changing experience.

In this particular scenario, I have to admit I'm struggling with the everything-happens-for-a-reason part. But what I do know is that Randi took my physical endurance and motivation to continue meeting my health and wellness goals to a whole other level. Continuing to meet these goals is up to me now, and so far, like with everything else in my life, although I don't always know what I'm doing, I accept the challenge.

You've now read stories about me on my best days, on my worst days, and days where my best isn't much better than my worst. But if you come away with anything after reading this book, I hope it is an understanding that days will come when you will be able to marvel at your resilience. It's not easy for someone with OCD to approach a situation with patience. To live life without "what if" scenarios—to not put proverbial carts before the horse when the horse hasn't even been hitched up yet. But there will be times when you surprise yourself, when this fortitude unearths itself from out of nowhere and you emerge as an even stronger, more remarkable individual than before, because *this* time you did demonstrate patience.

You will have times, like I did recently, when doing laundry you do decide to wash your clothes on warm instead of hot. Or when the warm cycle isn't working, and your clothes are in fact washed on cold instead of warm. You may, like me, scold yourself for deviating from a ritual that has always worked, and tell yourself, *See, that's exactly why you adopted that ritual in the first place.* You may, like me, consider this to be a situation of cataclysmic proportions that must be remedied by rewashing your clothes. But then, like me, you may tell yourself, *Stop it! What's the worst that can happen?* And you know what? After you're home for a few hours and are distracted watching your favorite program, you'll think a little bit less about it, and the next day, less than that, and the day after, even less than that.

Know that I get it and will always be there for you.

Even though I no longer wear the Converse All Stars featured in my wardrobe during middle school, or the Puma blue suede sneakers that got ruined during initiation, whatever pair of shoes I have on will always be like life: scuffed up, torn, with the soles peeling off. No matter what those shoes go through, or how hard they work, they will always have another story to tell.

Here is the first story I told to my writers group.

SHOES

October 2012

I had this piece all planned out. I was going to write about my shoes, how my identity is shaped by my shoes and my clothing, my obsessiveness over choosing just the right pair that defines me, and those perfect fits, which, once I do find them, look like six years of wear after six weeks. I was going to write an ode to my Converse All Stars and One Stars, which since middle school I have owned in every color from charcoal to chocolate, grape purple to orange. Well, more like puce, actually. And this homage to my clothes and shoes was going to be my magnum opus. These words, which were going to fly off the keyboard with such fluidity and eloquence, would channel every prolific writer and poet from Ogden Nash to Shel Silverstein, Walt Whitman to Susan Orlean.

I was going to write about my injury and how I have been forced to put my Chucks in the back of the closet, substituting them instead for geriatric wear that makes me look more like someone ready for assisted living rather than a young, healthy, thirty-something, single New Yorker. I was going to write about how I chose to wear the ratty Asics with the holes in them over the new and clean black New Balance sneakers that I bought in the hopes that I would find something cooler before the return window to the Super Runners Shop closed.

I was completely elated about the prospect of writing about all of this, and then election, phone banking and canvassing, choir rehearsals, production meetings, storm relief efforts, and of course, self-assessment deadlines hit—which, by the way, my friend Hilary, with a venomous look in her eye, said was a terrible excuse for not writing. So, instead of daffy and eloquent, you get thirty minutes of free writing and my promise and earnest commitment to do better next time.

DEAR READER,

On a final note: I sent this e-mail out to my friends a few weeks shy of my forty-first birthday. Now that we are friends—and you know pretty much everything about me—I'm hoping that you can help. Also, Roxy said I had to include this email somewhere in the book, that it was just too good not to share with my readers. And seriously, would you really want to cross Roxy? Remember what happened to that guy in chapter three!

Thank you in advance, and don't worry, that special prize applies to you as well. Especially if you can get me a date before I turn forty two!

**Please read this is not spam!!! I'm taking my
therapists challenge. Will you join me?**

Hi everyone,

Happy New Year!!! (Can you still wish people a happy new year in February?) One thing you all know about me is that I don't shy away from a challenge. Whether it's writing and publishing my first book, recovering from illness, or developing a healthy lifestyle, I approach it head on!

In a few weeks I will be turning 41, and while I have had many successes in my life both personally and professionally, there is one area in my life that remains a struggle . . . getting a damn date!!!

All kidding aside, even with my level of resourcefulness, figuring out how to enter a relationship still leaves me stymied.

Here's where you come in. I'm asking all of you to think about what you like about me. Is it my kind and generous nature, fierce passion as an activist, love of animals, ability to think critically and independently, salty self-deprecating sense of humor?

Maybe it isn't any of these things . . . maybe you don't really know why it is that were friends, but I want you to think about it, hard, for (at least) the next 48 hours, and after you've thought about it, I want you to comb through your address books and rolodex and find me a date!! Yes, that's right, you heard me correctly. I want you to find me a date. One date— for one coffee or a drink, just one date, nothing more and you will have fulfilled your mission.

For all of you who accept this challenge and take it seriously, I will award a prize, and trust me it will be good! I will put the same kind of thought into it that you put in for me. I will obsess over it and make this worth your while :)

I'm taking my therapist's challenge this year. Will you join me and make 41 the year that I bring it over the top?

Much love and gratitude,
Jen

ACKNOWLEDGMENTS

It should come as no surprise that the acknowledgements section is the part of this book I obsessed, worried, and procrastinated the most over.

The *what if* scenarios were flying at me so fast and hard they've been smacking me in the face for months now. *What if* I forget somebody? *What if* I acknowledge someone by their real name when they requested to be acknowledged under a pseudonym, an alias? *What if* I acknowledge someone by their full name, instead of just their first name? *What if* I acknowledge someone who specifically asked not to be acknowledged?! This would be the most the dire scenario of them all.

I have so many extraordinary people in my life that I want to thank, that if I did forget you, I would be subject to a lifetime of self-negation and berating myself over such a callous, egregious error.

So let's just say that if any of these scenarios do come up, and it's inevitable that they will, don't tell me! For due-diligence, here's one big THANK YOU to you all!

I want to end this book with a hopeful message, one that demonstrates growth and seeks to overcome some of my most challenging obsessive-compulsive behaviors. So, as a final exercise in achieving all these things, I am writing this acknowledgements section with zero semblance of order. Work friends will be mixed with activist friends, writers group with family members. It's going to drive me batty, but if it helps those who struggle with similar behaviors, I'm happy to do it—well, maybe not happy, but you get the point.

Okay, fine, there is one little piece of ordering information I need to include (Hey, listen, Rome wasn't built in a day, and it's for streamlining purposes only!): If your name appears with an asterisk next to it, you are part of both my work family, past or present, as well as writer's group family.

Thank you to Patchwork Farms Writing Retreat for being my respite and refuge while I was working on the draft manuscript. Thank you to Patricia Lee Lewis for always listening, never judging, teaching me how to tame the inner critic and creating a sacred place of healing where I could meet my deadlines while looking out at the Berkshire Mountains.

Thank you to DM Gordon for editing my draft manuscript and helping me to reach a point where I would be competition ready.

Thank you to *Keith Hoffman and *Hilary Tholen for pizza, wine, mood lamps, and creating the most important group I have ever been a part of. Thank you for sharing your voices and helping in more ways than I can name to shape mine!

Thank you to Selbern Narby and Barry Gliner for all the behind the scenes, operational tasks completed during and after hours at the office.

Thank you to *Danilo Alvarez, Wright Sibbald, and Jose Valera for technical support and web design.

Thank you to Alessandro Rafanelli and *Sarah Russell for taking photos for my headshots and making me look better than I ever have before. You were able to achieve magic under some seriously harrowing conditions. By the way, the essay is forthcoming!

Thank you to Charlie Foley—I'm actually not sure why, but he asked to be included and I'm a woman of my word.

Thank you to When Words Count Retreat and all the incredible staff. Steve Eisner for his vision. Charita Cole Brown and Peg Moran for coaching and editorial services. Thank you to all the extraordinary writers I met along the way for sharing their gifts and their voices, especially Mike Keren for his friendship and continued guidance.

Thank you to Lane Heymont and the Tobias Literary Agency.

Thank you to Meryl Moss and Meryl Moss Media for help with publicity.

Thank you to Green Writers Press. Especially my publisher, Dede Cummings, for believing in me, giving me this incredible opportunity, and getting excited when I refused too! It's an honor to be one of your authors.

Thank you to Ben Tanzer for creating the best marketing one sheet I could ever ask for, your enthusiasm, and being so generous with your time when you really didn't have to be.

Thank you to Sarah Ellis for her careful attention to detail and copy-editing expertise.

Thank you to Hannah Wood for her inventive book design.

Thank you to Asha Hossain for creating a cover design that attracts and entices readers from miles away.

Thank you to my fantastic editor, Rose Alexandre-Leach. I know she doesn't like to be in the spotlight, but she deserves to be! There aren't enough accolades in the English language to describe what you've done for me. Because of you, I'm a better writer now than I was when I first started this process. Thank you for your mentorship, friendship, and most importantly, for teaching me what the abbreviation DGATE means and making me promise never to do it again!

Thank you to Ruth for your friendship, being part of my story, and getting me through some very difficult times.

Thank you to all my activist friends. You know who you are. Thank you for your passion dedication, anger, and always understanding mine.

Thank you to Ellison Cavedo for being a jack of all trades. I know you'll be signing a copy of your book for me very soon!

Thank you to *Jamie Dugger. I cannot imagine what life would have been like without writers group. Years of passively nodding at each other in the hall, I guess, instead of dinners, weekend writing retreats at Patchwork, laughing, hugging, weeping. You once told me even if I castrated a camel, nothing I could say or do would ever change the way you think of me or our friendship. I am so eternally grateful for those words. Your friendship means everything. I hope someday we'll not only be sharing our writing over drinks but collaborating as well.

Thank you to *Roxy Nino. Hoo boy, where do I even start! Rox, if it wasn't for you, I'd probably be sitting in my old apartment on 8th Ave and Lincoln Place, rocking back and forth in a catatonic state with drool coming out of the side of my mouth. They would have needed a forklift to pry me off the floor and out onto the street. Thank you for not subjecting me and the city of New York to this. I owe you my life and would do anything for you. Just one more favor, though: stop sending cards! Valentine's Day, birthdays, St. Patrick's Day, Ground Hog Day—enough with the cards, Rox! I love them and you but I'm running out of room!

Thank you to Adeena, my extraordinary friend of twenty-five years and counting! It's hard for me to fathom what life would have been like if I hadn't met you and we hadn't been roommates. You and your mom were two of the first people to encourage me to keep writing, no matter what. Thank you to sweet Jonah and Ezra for making a cameo appearance in this book. You helped me to shape the ending to the story in more ways than you will ever know.

Thank you to my trainer, Johari Mayfield. You filled a gap in my health and wellness goals at a time when I needed it most. Instead of feeling like I was starting over, you made it a seamless transition.

Thank you to Robyn Landow, PhD, my therapist of fourteen years, for getting me this far, and for being a reader and proofing my clinical definitions for accuracy. Maybe now that I'm less than two months shy of publication, we can finally get back to talking about something else other than this book!

And last, but certainly not least, to my mom. Mumsy, this book is dedicated to you. Because what better way to communicate to you that you're not a disappointment as a mother.

And her wailing and whining kicking and screaming

  causes her salty tearical contents
     to t
         r
     on   i
      this   c
      BROWN   k
      BLOB   l
                  e

AND the liquid begins to
    BUBBLE
  The gravel
  PIERCING
  This floppy
  consistency
    AND
  The liquid
  from this
  FLOPPY
  GLOPPY
  BLOBBY
  GLOBBY
  consistency

  E*X*P*L*O*D*E*S

  like a geyser
  FLOODING
  the streets

    NOW
can you imagine this internally?
    Well I can.
       JENNY